C0-AVJ-288

How shall they hear?

Church-based evangelism

Peter Jeffery

 EVANGELICAL PRESS

EVANGELICAL PRESS
12 Wooler Street, Darlington, Co. Durham, DL1 1RQ, England.

© Evangelical Press 1996
First published 1996

British Library Cataloguing in Publication Data available

ISBN 0 85234 383 3

Printed and bound in Great Britain by Cox & Wyman, Reading.

Contents

Introduction

Evangelism is not primarily a matter of method and technique, but of a correct biblical attitude on the part of Christians. This book is not about evangelistic methods, though they will be touched upon. Its concern is rather to help believers see their God-given responsibility to evangelize a lost world. *How* we do it is nothing like as important as doing it. This is not to say that method is unimportant. Unfortunately, in recent years, much evangelistic effort has been so man-centred that it has produced countless 'decisions for Christ' but few true conversions to Christ. A method that does not see souls truly saved, but merely attracts and entertains sinners, is not biblical evangelism. The purpose of evangelism is to reach sinners with the gospel, so that they might come in repentance and faith to Christ.

One of the problems of the man-centred methods of the last forty years is that some Christians have been put off from doing any evangelism at all. Evangelical believers tend to swing from one extreme to another. We see bad, unbiblical methods being used and decide the safest thing to do is nothing. This attitude is just as wrong as a preoccupation with instant results. 'No evangelism' is not the answer to bad evangelism.

A correct attitude to evangelism will reflect three things, namely:

1. A concern for the glory of God;
2. A concern for lost souls;
3. A concern to be obedient to the commands of Christ.

Western civilization, in Europe and North America, has produced a culture that cares little or nothing for God. You only have to consider some of the things that are legally and socially acceptable today, like abortion and homosexuality, to see the truth of this. God no longer counts in the thinking of most people. The nominal Christianity propagated by religious programmes on the radio and TV demonstrates the same truth. For most religious people today biblical Christianity is a joke, an outdated theory that is no longer relevant, and being 'born again' has become a term of disdain.

Only one thing is going to change all this, and that is for men and women to be truly saved and made new in Christ. Once a man knows and experiences the joy of new (that is, spiritual) birth he will never again mock it. Once a sinner's eyes are opened to the beauty of Scripture it will be his delight for ever. One of the reasons why God saves sinners is that they might be to 'the praise of his glorious grace' (Eph. 1:6). Thus God is glorified in the salvation of everyone who comes to Christ. There are many other ways in which Christians can glorify God, but surely one of the greatest is to be used by God to proclaim the gospel of Christ through which alone sinners can be saved. It is no use mourning over the way the world thinks of God if we do nothing to make him real to men and women who are dead in their sins. Our first concern, then, must be for *the glory of God*.

Secondly, we must be concerned for *the souls of men*. Men and women without Christ as their Saviour are going to hell. They are not simply going to a 'Christless eternity', as it is often put. They are without Christ now. They are going to exist for ever under the wrath and judgement of a holy God. Christians often ask, 'How can I get a burden for souls?' The answer has to be: read the Bible and believe it. Believe what it has to say about the terror of the Lord and the eternity of judgement. Then consider that this is what your unbelieving children and parents and friends will have to face unless they turn to Christ. If that does not give you a burden for souls then nothing will. If unbelievers are to avoid hell they must be saved. There must be a genuine work of the Holy Spirit in their lives that transforms them by grace and justifies them by faith. If we believe this, then our methods of evangelism will be those which, as far as possible, avoid empty decisions. We want to see these folk truly saved, not just becoming religious for a short time.

Do you see how these two concerns will govern our attitude to evangelism and give it both relevance and urgency? So, thirdly, will a concern *to be obedient to the commands of Christ.* He has commanded us to go into all the world and tell out this gospel. Once our attitude is right, evangelism will become inevitable. We will not have to be persuaded and organized into periodic 'evangelistic campaigns', but will see evangelism as a privilege and joy.

1.
Go to all nations

One of the most important passages on evangelism in the New Testament is Acts chapter 11, where Peter recounts the conversion of Cornelius and his household, the first Gentile believers. The chapter also tells how the gospel was spread by believers who left Jerusalem on account of persecution, and how Paul was recruited by Barnabas to help in the work at Antioch. Our first four chapters will draw heavily upon the rich fund of teaching and example on our subject provided by Acts 11.

Almost the last words of Jesus to his disciples before the ascension were: 'Go and make disciples of all nations' (Matt. 28:19). He told them, 'You will be my witnesses in Jerusalem, and in all Judea and Samaria, and to the ends of the earth' (Acts 1:8). This was a divine command and with it went the promise of the power of the Holy Spirit to enable them to carry out this crucial work. But the command was not at first obeyed. The apostles and the other believers had seen the power of the resurrection, they had been filled with the Holy Spirit at Pentecost and seen thousands converted, but all that took place in and around Jerusalem and within the Jewish community. No effort was made initially to spread the gospel to the Gentiles. The first Christians were Jews, and most Jews had a deeply rooted prejudice against non-Jews.

They thought that God was only interested in them and found it difficult to understand that people of other nationalities could also benefit from the grace of God. Remember that these were men filled with the Holy Spirit. They had been used mightily by God. Yet because of this prejudice they had no great desire to spread the gospel to other nations. We all need to seek the fulness of the Spirit, and long for more of the Spirit's power in our lives, but let us not be so foolish as to think that this will make all our weaknesses and problems disappear. That was not the case in New Testament times and never has been since.

Even a man filled with the Holy Spirit can be wrong unless he heeds the Word of God. If these men had listened to Jesus when he told them to go to all nations they would have seen that the gospel was for everyone. But their actions were affected by their prejudices and this threatened to hinder the work of evangelism.

Hindrances to evangelism today

The prejudice of believers held back evangelism by the early church and it still does today. Consider some of the attitudes among evangelicals that put a brake upon effective evangelism.

1. Doctrinal prejudices

Doctrinal prejudices can be a real problem. Admittedly, this is not too widespread, but even the Calvinism of some Christians gets in the way of a biblical outreach. They say, 'If God is going to save the elect he will do it without our help. Therefore there is no need to evangelize.' I knew one very sincere believer who would not pray for his parents' salvation because he was not sure if they were among the elect.

The doctrine of divine election to salvation is profoundly biblical and dear to the heart of well-taught believers. But properly understood it ought to inspire evangelism, not frustrate it. In Romans 9 Paul spells out this doctrine very clearly. Salvation does not depend, says verse 16, on man's desire or effort, but solely on God's mercy. In the next chapter, however, the apostle declares equally clearly that no one can be saved without hearing the gospel (Rom. 10:14-15), and that none will hear unless we go and tell them. Even though a man be chosen in Christ before the foundation of the world (Eph. 1:4), he cannot be saved unless he hears the gospel. God ordains not only the end of salvation but also the means. Another offshoot of this doctrinal prejudice is a reluctance to make a free offer of the gospel to all men. Yet Christ commanded us to preach the gospel to 'every creature' (Mark 16:15, NKJV).

2. *A lack of concern*

Do we care enough for the souls of men and women, or are we indifferent to their salvation? Do we really believe in hell? If one of us had a young child in our family with some terminal illness we would be terribly grieved. We would feel the matter deeply and be unable to put it out of our minds. This is right and proper: it is a response governed by love and real concern. We would get our Christian friends to pray for the loved one and plead with God for healing. Physical death is real to us all and we feel its pangs and pain. But somehow eternal death is not so real to us. We all have loved ones who are living without Christ and who will go to hell if they die in that condition, but we rarely shed a tear for their souls. As long as the death of the body seems more important to us than spiritual death, evangelism will always lack the urgency that characterizes New Testament life and witness. This is not to say that the believer should become depressed over the state of the unsaved, for he should be filled with 'joy and peace in believing'. But there should be a godly concern for the lost.

3. *Past failures*

The end of the twentieth century is a hard time for biblical Christianity and this has created in believers an acute sense of disappointment with past evangelistic efforts. The sentiments of many are: 'What is the use of telling sinners about Jesus when no one will listen? We see so few conversions that we have stopped expecting them.'

In many ways this attitude is understandable and one sympathizes with the disappointment of Christians frustrated with their past failures. But those who think in this way are forgetting the sovereignty of God and revealing an ignorance of church history. So often in the past, times of acute spiritual darkness have been followed by rich blessing. What a dark time it was for Israel with that wicked man Herod on the throne — with their God-given land ruled by the armies of pagan Rome, and with their God-given religion sucked dry by the legalism and pride of the Pharisees! To any godly soul the situation must have seemed dark and hopeless. Yet at that very moment God sent Jesus into the world.

The same lesson has been evident all through the history of the church. In 1721 Erasmus Saunders wrote *A View of the State of Religion in the Diocese of St David's*. He said that in West Wales, 'So many of our churches are in actual ruins; so many more are almost ready to fall.'[1] Saunders went on to say that some men ordained to the church were practically illiterate, and far from being spiritually called, had entered the ministry because they were unlikely to succeed in any other profession. Growing up not far from St Davids at this awful time were nine-year-old Daniel Rowland and eight-year-old Howell Harris, and within a short time God used these young men to turn the land upside down spiritually. What God did then he can do again: times of little response are no reason to suspend the work of the gospel, but should instead prompt a greater sense of urgency.

4. The fear of man

If we were honest with ourselves we would admit that one
of the greatest hindrances to personal evangelism is fear.
The fear of being laughed at and ridiculed by unbelieving
friends and relatives puts many Christians in bondage. In
many ways this fear is understandable, and most of us
suffer from it to some degree. We do not want to be the
'odd one out', and life is much more pleasant if we are
popular with others. The old saying, 'Sticks and stones
may break my bones but words can never hurt me,' is just
not true. The bruises caused by being called 'a fanatic' or
'old-fashioned' can take a lot longer to heal than those
caused by sticks and stones. All through the New Testament we read how Christ and his followers had to face this
kind of treatment. For example:

> John the Baptist was accused of having 'a de-
> mon' (Matt. 11:18);
> Jesus was branded a glutton and a drunkard
> (Matt. 11:19);
> People were offended by what Jesus said (Mark
> 6:3);
> People made fun of the early Christians (Acts
> 2:13);
> Paul was said to be 'out of his mind' (Acts
> 26:24);

and so we could continue. The same has been true right
through church history. So how did Christians cope with
this?

First of all, they got things in perspective and acknowledged that their first priority was to please God and not men (Acts 5:29; Gal. 1:10). Once this was set in their minds they were able to rejoice 'because they had been counted worthy of suffering disgrace for the Name' (Acts 5:41). This did not give them a martyr's complex, but it did mean they were willing to become fools for Christ's sake. The only way to rid yourself of the fear of what men think and say is to be so absorbed in Christ that pleasing him supersedes everything else.

5. Waiting for revival

Many believers quite rightly have a great longing for revival. For years they have prayed to God to pour out his Holy Spirit upon our land as he has done in other times in the history of the church. This longing is fuelled by accounts of the extraordinary activity of God in revival, when more may be accomplished by a single sermon than by a hundred such sermons in ordinary times. Such longing must be right. But if it regards anything short of revival as useless, and judges evangelism to be a waste of time, then it can actually become a hindrance to the work of God. Only God can revive our nation, but he has commanded *us* to evangelize it. A genuine longing for revival should produce a corresponding concern to reach people with the gospel of God's grace in Christ.

How God deals with hindrances

The Jewish prejudice was so deep-rooted in the thinking of God's people that in order to remove it he had to do two remarkable things. First of all, he gave a special vision to Peter (see Acts 10:1-23) to get him to go and preach to the Roman, Cornelius. Peter's prejudice is clearly spelt out in Acts 10:28, and it is evident from Acts 11:2-3 that this attitude was shared by many of his fellow-believers. Using Peter's account of the conversion of the Gentiles, God dealt firmly with these wrong attitudes, so that eventually the whole church was constrained to confess, 'So then, God has granted even the Gentiles repentance unto life' (Acts 11:18). This was a remarkable break-through, leading to a new understanding of the breadth of divine love and grace.

However, to understand something is not the same as to practise it. The second thing God did, therefore, was to make sure that they spread the gospel abroad by using persecution to get them out of Jerusalem (Acts 11:19). Even then, as we read at the end of verse 19, they at first preached the message of Christ only to Jews. They seemed blind to the glaring inconsistency between their declaration in verse 18 and their limited vision in verse 19. The difference between these two verses is the difference between what we acknowledge to be true and what we actually do. We can apply this principle to many aspects of our Christian life, but let us confine ourselves here to the context of evangelism. It is not enough to have a theoretical belief in the evangelization of the world. We must actually get on with the work in our own backyard! Surely no Bible-believing Christian can doubt that when Jesus told the first believers to be his witnesses, he was speaking as much to us as to them. Every Christian in every generation is to be a witness for the Lord Jesus Christ.

Life and word

There are two ways in which we witness — by life and by word. Jesus said, 'Let your light shine before men, that they may see your good deeds and praise your Father in heaven' (Matt. 5:16). When we become Christians we are converted, which means that we are changed. That change must be seen. The standards of human society in relation to honesty, truth and morality are so abysmally low that any Christian's life ought to stand out.

When we think of evangelism we tend almost exclusively to think of methods, whereas the New Testament is more concerned with the sanctified life of the believer. We need to be usable by God. If you went into a restaurant and they served your meal on dirty crockery you would refuse to eat it. In the same way God will not use dirty vessels. He wants us clean and holy and this is where we should start in evangelism. 'As he who called you is holy, so be holy in all you do' (1 Peter 1:15). To be holy means having a close walk with God. A. W. Tozer points out that we make a fundamental mistake if we tell new converts that the first thing they need to learn is how to witness. No,

said Tozer, the first thing they need to learn is to worship.[2]
In other words, if their relationship with God is right, then
witness will follow naturally.

So get your life with God right; that is where evangelism starts. But it does not end there. Paul argues that
unbelievers cannot be saved unless someone tells them
the gospel (Rom. 10:14-15). Therefore witness by word
is crucial. An unbeliever may be able to live an admirable
life, but only a Christian can speak of Jesus and his
salvation. In evangelism both life and word are necessary. Life is important because it gives substance and
conviction to what we say. Why should anyone listen to
us when we talk of the Lord if the way we live contradicts
what we say? Your Christian life is important, but no one
is saved only by seeing how we live, for faith comes by
hearing. Your Christian life will tell the world where you
stand, but it needs your words to tell them where they
stand. There is a temptation, perhaps, to think that my life
is my witness and I have no need to say anything. The
Bible does not substantiate that idea. Both life and word
are necessary if our evangelism is to be true to Scripture.

2.
The messengers and their message

Once the prejudice against non-Jews was dealt with by God, the Christians began at last to fulfil the Lord's command to go to all nations. Thus we read in Acts 11:20 that they began to witness to Greeks. Note that these witnesses were unknown, nameless believers. There was no Peter or Paul or Philip or any great preacher in sight at that stage. It was just ordinary Christians who were evangelizing and their method was simply to tell the good news concerning the Lord Jesus Christ.

Three things are essential to the spreading of the gospel, and if any one of these is missing then, whatever else you have, you do not have evangelism. These essentials are:

1. The good news about the Lord Jesus;
2. Christians to tell it;
3. Unbelievers to hear it.

Furthermore, if evangelism is to be successful, a fourth ingredient is needed. This we see in Acts 11:21: 'The Lord's hand was with them.' That is, the mighty power of God accompanied the telling of the message of salvation, and we shall look at this in the chapter that follows.

Unorganized evangelism

How did they 'tell the message'? Was it by preaching to groups of unbelievers, or by one-to-one personal witness? Probably it was a mixture of both, with an emphasis on the latter because there are no preachers mentioned by name. Today we have a tendency to think of evangelism as a special effort organized every couple of years with an imported evangelist to do the telling for us. There has to be a place for this in the life of the church but it is no substitute for the unorganized evangelism of Acts 11.

The great danger of organized evangelism, whether it be a large campaign or door-to-door visitation by the local church, is that when the special effort is over we think that is the end of it until next time. But the biblical concept is that witness is something for every day and for every Christian. This is by far the most effective kind of evangelism. Great claims are made for mass evangelism but it is now accepted that few of the hundreds who 'go forward' at such meetings continue to profess the Christian faith for long. Also, few today are converted through door-to-door evangelism or open-air preaching. You can test this statement quite easily by asking yourself how many Christians you know who were saved through door-to-door visitation or open-air meetings. Most people first hear the gospel through one of two channels:

the Christian home or the personal witness of a friend. These are the prime channels through which sinners today are brought under the sound of the gospel. They may then, of course, be taken to church to hear the Word of God preached in a more formal context, so that preaching is by no means sidelined in this scenario. But the initial contact is often not church attendance except, perhaps, for the children of a Christian family.

This does not mean that we stop using the more traditional means of evangelism, but it emphasizes that the most effective evangelism is unorganized. It happens as the individual believer goes to his or her place of work, or circle of relatives and friends, and speaks of Christ; as Christians pass on suitable literature, or invite unbelievers to a preaching service at their church. It is what has been called 'gossiping the gospel'. Some Christians find this difficult to do, but the remedy for this failing is that we should start talking to one another about Christ! It is sad how little Christ comes into the conversation between Christians. If we cannot talk to one another about the Lord, we shall never be able to talk to unbelievers.

Telling the good news

In Acts 11:19-20 the evangelism of the early church is very simply described as telling the people 'the good news about the Lord Jesus'. They preached, proclaimed, heralded, declared, or stated the truth about Jesus. There was no hesitation, nor was the message watered down. Their evangelism was not half-hearted or reluctant. They

believed that without Jesus people would go to hell, and
this added a note of urgency to their message. But they
also believed that before time began God, in love and
mercy, had purposed to save a great multitude that no man
could number. This added a note of joy and confidence to
their message.

The early church was a telling church. Why was this?
Were not music and drama available as means of communication in the society of their day? Yes, but telling or
preaching was God's way of communicating the gospel,
and it still is. The principle presented in Romans 10:14-
15 is still relevant: how can they believe unless they hear,
and how can they hear without someone preaching to
them?

Somehow we have come to believe that telling or
preaching the good news about Jesus is the work of the
pulpit, while personal evangelism consists primarily in
sharing our testimony with unbelievers. It must be good
for Christians to give their testimony to non-Christians,
but unless that testimony is accompanied by a clear, even
if simple, declaration of who Jesus is and what he has
done for sinners, then the testimony will have the wrong
effect. It will make men look at us, rather than to Christ,
or else our story will be dismissed as some mystical
experience: 'That's fine for you, but not relevant for me.'
It is the truth about Jesus that puts men and women 'on the
spot' and forces them to think seriously about themselves
and God. Even though all Christians cannot be preachers
in the pulpit sense, we are all meant to tell the good news
about the Lord Jesus.

Preaching Christ

So much, then, for the messengers. But what is the *message* of evangelism? The purpose of the gospel is to bring rebel sinners to God, and make them his children and heirs. Through the gospel they are born anew, forgiven, reconciled, accepted and adopted, all in Christ. Though some trust in morality and good works, and others in philosophy and religion, the fact is that only Jesus Christ can make us accepted by a holy God. It is crucial that we are clear about this in our thinking. The Word of God says that Jesus Christ is the only way to God. That is the uniform teaching of Scripture, as exemplified by Jesus (John 14:6), Peter (Acts 4:12) and Paul (1 Tim. 2:5). It is not being broad-minded and tolerant to say that all religions are the same and that all roads lead to God. To say that is to call Jesus a liar, for his claims are exclusive. The New Testament will not allow us to think otherwise and God will not condone such teaching. The evangelism of the early church clearly told sinners that 'There is no other name under heaven given to men by which we must be saved' (Acts 4:12).

We shall not be surprised, therefore, to learn that the message of New Testament evangelism is Christ himself. If we could ask Paul what he preached, he would reply that he preached 'Jesus Christ and him crucified' (1 Cor. 2:2). God had chosen him to 'preach him [Christ] among the Gentiles' (Gal. 1:16), and the apostle considered it an enormous privilege to preach 'the unsearchable riches of Christ' (Eph. 3:8). What is it, then, to 'preach Christ'? It is to proclaim who he is and what he has done.

Who is Jesus?

In Acts 11:20-24 Jesus is called 'Lord' several times. The name or title 'Lord' originated in the Old Testament. There God is called Yahweh or Jehovah, but the Jews thought this name to be so holy that they would not pronounce it. Instead they often substituted another word, the Hebrew word *Adonai*, meaning 'Lord'. This is one of the great Old Testament names for God. So to say that Jesus is Lord is simply to say that Jesus Christ is God. This is why Paul is able to say in Phillipians 2:10-11 that every knee will bow at the name of Jesus, a form of worship ascribed in the Old Testament only to Jahweh (see Isa. 45:23). This is so because Jesus is Lord; he is God. Notice in Acts 11:8 Peter, speaking to God the Father, calls him Lord. Then in verse 16 speaking of Jesus he also calls him Lord. As far as Peter is concerned there are not two Lords, not two Gods. Jesus is Lord because Jesus is God.

When the early church preached Jesus as Lord they declared boldly to the world that Jesus is God. And they had ample proof of this in the fulfilment of the Old Testament prophecies in the life of Jesus. The virgin birth, the miracles and the resurrection all underlined who Jesus is. There can be no evangelism without this basic biblical truth being declared as the foundation of everything else. People need to see that the gospel is not one way among many; it is not merely the opinion of Christians; it is the Word of the living God. To preach Jesus as Lord emphasizes this.

The doctrines of the substitutionary death of Christ and his bodily, physical resurrection are beyond belief to the natural man. And, indeed, they *are* impossible if Jesus was no more than a man, even the greatest man who ever lived. But Jesus is God and nothing is impossible to God. It is the lordship of Christ that gives substance and credence to the gospel. What Jesus did for us is only of significance because of who he is. For him to claim that he gave his life as a ransom for many, and that he died as a sinless substitute in the place of sinners, would be the height of arrogance if Jesus were not God.

What did Jesus do?

If you were to ask the apostle Peter, 'What did Jesus do?', this would be his answer: 'Christ died for sins once for all, the righteous for the unrighteous, to bring you to God' (1 Peter 3:18). This is the heart of the gospel that people need to hear. This is God's eternal plan of salvation. Jesus did not do these things because he was compelled by circumstances. Neither was his action the result of his own thinking and desire. He said that he came to do the will of his Father in heaven. The cross was planned in eternity by God, and in time God laid our sin upon his Son and punished those sins in him. Death, the wages of sin, smote the sinner's substitute, in order that the sinner might live to God. Christ was 'made ... to be sin' that we might wear his righteousness (2 Cor. 5:21).

We all, like sheep, have gone astray,
  each of us has turned to his own way;
and the Lord has laid on him
  the iniquity of us all

                                         (Isa. 53:6).

Apart from this there is no gospel and no hope for guilty sinners.

Christ died. But he also rose again from the dead 'for our justification' (Rom. 4:25). His resurrection declared that his offering for sin had been accepted, that God's justice had been satisfied and that sin and death had been conquered. Risen, ascended and seated at 'the right hand of the Majesty in heaven', he is able to 'save completely those who come to God through him' (Heb. 1:3; 7:25).

What, then, did Christ accomplish on the cross? He redeemed his elect, once and for all, so that there is now no further sacrifice for sin. He did not just make salvation possible, as many teach. His work of redemption was a perfect, finished work by which he secured the sure and eternal salvation of all those his Father gave him before time began. He defeated sin, Satan and death itself, that he might set his people free and become 'the firstborn among many brothers' (Rom. 8:29). This is what Jesus did and this is the message of evangelism. The gospel is the good news of what God has done for us in Christ. And because God alone has done it, it is a perfect, infallible and eternal work. It cannot fail, now or ever. There can be no evangelism without these truths.

3.
The hand of the Lord
in evangelism

Biblical truth is indispensable to evangelism but it is not in itself enough. The aim of the gospel is not only to teach sinners the truth; pre-eminently it is to save them, and something else is needed if sinners are to believe and be saved. We are told in Acts 11:21 that at Antioch 'A great number of people believed,' and there were two causes of this. There was the faithful witness of the Christians and there was the power of God using that witness to convict and convert sinners. William Arnot, a Scottish preacher of the nineteenth century wrote, 'The instrument is all human, but the power is all Divine. We learn here with great simplicity and clarity these two things; (1) that in conversion the hand of the Lord operates; but (2) that it operates through the ministry of men. In this work men can do nothing without God; but in this work God will do nothing without men.'[1]

It is not that God cannot do anything without men but that he chooses to use men in the work of salvation. Paul sets out the basic principle in 1 Corinthians 3:5-9. He describes himself and other preachers as 'servants, through whom you came to believe'. One servant planted the seed, another watered it, 'but God made it grow'. In the work of evangelism, Christians have the amazing privilege of being 'God's fellow-workers'. We see this principle in action in Acts 10 and 11. An angel appeared to Cornelius, not to preach the gospel to him but to tell him to send for Peter: 'He will bring you a message through which you and all your household will be saved' (Acts 11:14). God uses men to evangelize, not angels. But the point is also made in Acts 11:15 that the faithful witness of men, though crucial, is not enough: 'As I began to speak, the Holy Spirit came on them.' Men are taken into partnership with God, but the power that saves is God's alone.

What is divine power?

A. W. Tozer in his book *Paths to Power* defines what he means by power: 'First, I mean spiritual energy of sufficient voltage to produce great saints again. The breed of mild, harmless Christians grown in our generation is but a poor sample of what the grace of God can do when it operates in power in a human heart. Secondly, I mean a spiritual unction that will give a heavenly unction to our worship, that will make our meeting places sweet with the divine Presence. Then I mean that heavenly quality which marks the Church as a divine thing. Again, I mean that effective energy which God has, both in Biblical and in post-Biblical times, released into the Church and into the circumstances surrounding her, which made her fruitful in labour and invincible before her foes. Lastly, by power

I mean that divine afflatus [inspiration] which moves the heart and persuades the hearer to repent and believe in Christ.'

After listing these things Tozer concludes by saying, 'Everything else being equal, we shall have as much success in Christian work as we have power, no more and no less. Lack of fruit over a period argues lack of power as certainly as the sparks fly upwards. Outward circumstances may hinder for a time, but nothing can long stand against the naked power of God. As well try to fight the jagged lightning as to oppose this power when it is released upon men. Then it will either save or destroy; it will give life or bring death.'[2]

Again and again, both the Bible and the history of the church record how this power was demonstrated in the past, both in preaching and the everyday witness of God's people. The many revivals which the church has been privileged to experience historically show us this power in a remarkable degree, but it is seen even outside of revival. Not a single soul could be saved apart from God's power. Let us therefore examine this power in relation to four essential aspects of the Christian's life.

Power and preaching

When Paul evangelized the city of Corinth, he tells us, his preaching was 'not with wise and persuasive words, but with a demonstration of the Spirit's power'. This was important, for he did not want their faith to 'rest on men's wisdom, but on God's power' (1 Cor. 2:1-5). No doubt

Paul could have gained a following by preaching what men wanted to hear, by an eloquent appeal to their intellects, or by offering them various inducements to believe. But this he spurned. Nothing but the power of the Holy Spirit could create new spiritual life in those dead in trespasses and sins. Only this power could raise men from spiritual death to life in Christ. Only people 'born from above' would hold fast to their profession of faith.

We also need to rely upon the Spirit of God for results. It is always tempting to try to entice people by gimmicks and entertainments, to attempt to build the church by human methods rather than divine power. All such attempts, however, are doomed to failure. The only results that will glorify God and endure to the end are those which flow from the work of the Holy Spirit in our hearers. We are utterly dependent upon him.

Power and prayer

In Acts 11 there is no mention of the believers praying before they evangelized, but the whole account starts in verse 9 of the previous chapter with Peter at prayer. This prayer time was not a matter of the apostle pleading with God for the souls of Gentiles, but of God dealing with his servant. It is often said that prayer changes things, but this is chiefly true if the prayer first changes the Christian who is praying. Peter's prayer did change things dramatically, but only because it first changed his attitude to evangelism. The prayer led to the vision; the vision led to Peter preaching to Cornelius; and this paved the way for other believers to witness to the Greeks. Then the power of God came and a great number believed.

Prayer is not about us persuading a reluctant God to do what we think is right. Nor does the power of prayer depend on how many Christians we can get to pray. If one saint or a million pray for something that is outside the will of God, it will avail nothing. Perhaps we spend too much time in prayer asking for things and not enough time dwelling on who God is and seeking to know his purposes. To quote Tozer again, 'In all our praying, however, it is important that we keep in mind that God will not alter his eternal purposes at the word of a man. We do not pray in order to persuade God to change his mind. Prayer is not an assault upon the reluctance of God, nor an effort to secure a suspension of his will for us or for those for whom we pray. Prayer is not intended to overcome God and "move his arm". God will never be other than himself, no matter how many people pray, nor how long nor how earnestly. What the praying man does is to bring his will into line with the will of God so God can do what he has all along been willing to do. Thus prayer changes the man and enables God to change things in answer to man's prayer.'[3]

This does not mean that we should not plead with God to save souls, but it does mean that we must use prayer to commune with God, to praise him, to delight in him, to worship him and to learn from him what and when he wants things done. This creates a deeper knowledge of God which produces a greater awareness of his power and a greater expectancy in us to see this power at work. It also leads to something of the heart and mind of God being

fashioned in us. Then, like our Saviour, we shall weep for
souls. Such weeping will not be merely a demonstration
of emotion on our part, but a reflection of the sentiments
of God. When this takes place we can expect to see divine
power saving the lost.

Power and effort

The salvation of a soul is a work of divine love, grace and
power. Love and grace would not be enough without the
power. In Ephesians 1:19-20 Paul likens the power of
God needed to save a soul to 'the working of his mighty
strength, which he exerted in Christ when he raised him
from the dead'. The staggering thing is that, even with
such mighty power at work, God still requires that the
effort of Christians be involved. We have seen from
Scripture that evangelism is our work, not that of angels,
and in it we are God's fellow-workers. Acts 11:21 re-
emphasizes this: 'The Lord's hand was with them.' The
power of God did not work in isolation from the efforts of
the believers. The same is true throughout the book of
Acts. The Ethiopian in chapter 8 was an earnest seeker
who had the Scriptures, but he still needed Philip to
explain the gospel to him. There is no doubt that God
could have saved this man by allowing him to read and
understand the Scripture without the help of Philip. There
have been many examples of this, but God's normal way
is to use his people to reach the lost.

This is a tremendous privilege for us, but it is also a
great responsibility. Evangelism requires effort. God

does not bless laziness and indolence. It is no use praying for God to speak to your neighbour if you are not prepared to speak to that person yourself about Christ. The effort God requires from us is to start where we are. In the language of Acts 1, we must evangelize Jerusalem, Judea and Samaria before going to the ends of the earth. In biblical terms it does not make sense to go to a part of your town where you are not known, to evangelize by knocking at the doors of strangers, if you are not talking to the people in your own street about the Saviour. It is not effort for the sake of effort that God requires, but effort that stems from a deep concern to see individuals saved.

Power and obedience

Jesus said to his apostles that they would receive power when the Holy Spirit came to them (Acts 1:8), and Peter tells us that God gives the Holy Spirit to those who obey him (Acts 5:32). From these two verses it is a reasonable deduction that without the Holy Spirit there is no power, and without obedience we shall not know the full glories of the indwelling Spirit. Thus, failure to obey the revealed will of God will mean no fulness of the Spirit in our lives and little power. Power in evangelism is not the result of good organization and strong personalities exercising their natural abilities. The power that saves dead souls is exclusively and uniquely God's. If we want to see that power at work we must begin, not with methods, but with lives lived in obedience to the Word of God.

Jesus himself gives prominence to obedience both by his example and his teaching, and we dare not ignore it. 'I have come ... not to do my will,' he said, 'but the will of him who sent me' (John 6:38). The obedience he gave to his Father, and the obedience he expects from us, is not promoted by fear or selfish ambition, but by love (John 14:15). There can be no effective service for God without obedience, and if we want to know what obedience is and what it involves we have to look at Christ. In his life and witness we see that true obedience involves communion with the Father. It is not merely following a set of rules. It is very interesting and certainly not without significance that the expression 'obey the commandments' is very seldom used in Scripture; it is almost always 'obey me' or 'obey my voice'.

In other words, obedience and communion are twins. What we are to obey is not some impersonal list of dos and don'ts but the voice of God. Obedience flows out of love for God and an awareness of his nearness. Evangelism without this love and awareness is merely going through the motions, however well-intentioned, and it will be devoid of saving power.

Power and sanctification

It has been said that the church has never had so many gadgets and gimmicks as it has today, and has never been so powerless. There is sufficient truth in this to remind us of a greatly neglected element in effective evangelism, namely the sanctified lives of believers. Robert Murray

M'Cheyne linked the holiness of the believer with effective evangelism when he said, 'I feel there are two things it is impossible to desire with sufficient ardour: personal holiness and the honour of Christ in the salvation of souls.'[4] David Brainerd felt the same way: 'There was nothing of any importance to me but holiness of heart and life and the conversion of the Indians to God.'[5]

To be sanctified is to be set apart for God's use and glory. It is to be, in some measure, like Christ. This is only possible because we have also been justified in God's sight. Justification means that God accepts us in Christ, and sanctification suits us for his use. Union with the Lord Jesus Christ is the foundation of sanctification. He is became for us 'righteousness, and sanctification and redemption' (1 Cor. 1:30, NKJV). It is because we are in Christ that we are called to be like Christ. The sanctified life of the believer is important to evangelism for two reasons.

First of all, see it from the unbeliever's viewpoint. Non-Christians are not fools and they can tell whether what we say is contradicted by how we live. If our life does not match our words then the words will be rejected. It is no use telling unbelievers not to look at you but at Jesus. Such language is incomprehensible to them. All they can see is you, and they will judge the validity of your message by the impact it is making on your own life. A holy life is a powerful message and difficult to refute.

Secondly, a holy life pleases and glorifies God. If our lives are sanctified we can be of great use to God in evangelism even though we could never preach a sermon. Personality and speaking ability are not as important as a

life that pleases God. Paul reminds the Corinthians how
he came to them: 'I came to you in weakness and fear, and
with much trembling. My message and my preaching
were not with wise and persuasive words' (1 Cor. 2:3-4).
Would your church invite an evangelist like that to con-
duct a campaign for you? But Paul goes on to say that his
ministry was 'with a demonstration of the Spirit's
power'. The result was that many souls were saved and a
church was established at Corinth. Clearly the reason for
this was that God was pleased to pour upon Paul the glorious power of the Holy Spirit. He could not have done so
unless Paul had been seeking to live a life that honoured
God and exalted the Lord Jesus Christ.

Paul is not telling us in these verses that the use of
natural gifts of oratory is wrong. Through the centuries
God has been pleased to give his church great preachers
like Charles Spurgeon, George Whitefield and many
others. What he is saying is that these men spoke with
power because they did not trust in their natural talents
but in the power of God. Thus they sought to live for his
glory.

Sanctification does not mean sinless perfection: if that
were the case all evangelism would be a miserable failure.
It means seeking to be like Christ in all things, even
though we often fail. With Robert Murray M'Cheyne, we
will pray, 'Lord, make me as holy as a pardoned sinner
can be.'

4.
The fruit of evangelism

The fruit of evangelism is saved souls. But how are we to know if someone is genuinely converted? Warren Wiersbe makes the strong point that 'There is a difference between "fruit" and "results". You can get "results" by following sure-fire formulas, manipulating people, or turning on your charisma; but "fruit" comes from life. When the Spirit of life is working through the Word of life, the seed planted bears fruit; and that fruit has in it the seeds for more fruit (Genesis 1:11-12). Results are counted and soon become silent statistics, but living fruit remains and continues to multiply to the glory of God (John 15:6).'[1]

It is obvious both from the New Testament and our own experience that not all who profess faith in Christ are truly converted. In Acts 8 we are told of a man who believed and was baptized. Yet soon after, the apostle Peter tells him that his heart is not right before God and that he is full of bitterness and captive to sin. Previous to this, in the parable of the sower, the Lord Jesus himself had warned of the possibility of false professions. Some people receive the gospel warmly but they last only a short time because there is no root in them, that is, no real experience of Christ (Mark 4:17).

A serious problem

False profession is a very serious problem. It is serious for the people who make a profession of faith that is not real. They may be told they are Christians but it is soon obvious that they are not. Often such people become so disillusioned with the Christian faith that they become almost impossible to reach with further evangelism. Several years ago I was preaching in an open-air meeting in the local market. All the time our meeting was going on a young man stood nearby selling *Communist Workers'* newspapers. After we had finished I went to speak to him and during our conversation he firmly told me that Christianity was a fraud, because it did not work. He was convinced of this, he said, because he had once been a Christian. He had been 'saved' by going forward at a large crusade meeting and he had a decision card to prove it. But after a short time he realized, so he said, that he had been deceived. Becoming a Christian (as he thought) had changed nothing in his life so he had become a Communist instead. Nothing I could say to him touched him. He was hard and unyielding in his opposition to the gospel.

It is also serious for the church, which may be thanking God in prayer and praise for a person's conversion one day, only to find that within a short time the 'new convert' is back in the world and rarely if ever seen in church. This sort of experience can easily demoralize and discourage believers in their evangelistic efforts.

It is serious too for nominal Christians, those good churchgoers who are always in church but have never been saved. They are actually encouraged in their nominalism when they see false professions. What happens is this. Someone in the church is claimed to have been saved. He or she is encouraged to give a testimony but before long stops attending the Sunday services. The nominal Christian sees this as showing how meaningless is all this business of being saved. He or she says, 'I have never had a conversion experience but I'm still in church, unlike so-and-so.'

A solution

False professions of faith are a serious problem in all sorts of ways, but the worst thing about them is that they bring dishonour to the name of God. So how do we solve this dilemma?

First of all, we must acknowledge that the problem will never disappear altogether. If it occurred during the revival in Samaria described in Acts 8, it will also occur in our less spiritually enlightened days. That is a fact but it is no excuse for indifference. We must try to reduce drastically the number of times it happens.

One way to do this is to examine biblically our methods of evangelism. If we substitute an 'easy believism' which only requires an intellectual agreement with certain gospel truths for the New Testament demand for repentance and faith, then shallow, superficial 'conversions' will abound. The decision system practised in much modern evangelicalism aggravates the problem. This system, which was unknown until the early nineteenth century, has become for many an indispensable part of evangelism. Indeed many people think that they become Christians merely by 'going forward' at an evangelistic meeting. To be fair, some evangelists are careful to say this is not so, but because of the widespread use of the practice people still think it is the only way to be saved. (For a more detailed study on this subject see *The Decision System* by Iain Murray, published by the Banner of Truth Trust).

In recent years amazing claims have been made of the thousands who are alleged to be saved through mass evangelism. Everyone knows that not all who go forward are truly converted, but it is argued that if only a fraction are genuine then the method is justified. I can understand the sentiments behind this argument, but the New Testament will not allow us to forget the others, namely those thousands who were told they were Christians, thought they were Christians, but soon became disillusioned because in reality they were nothing of the kind. The damage is enormous and unnecessary. It is caused, not by the gospel, but by a system of evangelism that has no biblical foundation.

This kind of thing is not confined to mass evangelism. It also happens at summer camps and in local churches. How do we deal with it? We need to be more careful about publicly labelling a profession of faith as a conversion. Professions can be the result of several things: emotionalism, pressure from friends, sincere desires, or plain deceit. True conversion is always and only produced by the convicting and regenerating work of the Holy Spirit, in which the gifts of repentance and faith are imparted to the soul. Our forefathers used to make a distinction between a soul awakened and a soul converted. Profession of faith is sometimes the premature response of an awakened heart. Of course, if God begins a work in someone's heart, he will surely bring it to completion. However, impatient for results, we may mistake mere concern or interest for the work of the Spirit, and so encourage a profession from one who is not regenerate.

Several years ago we had a magnificent crop of apples from the trees in our garden and were determined to save as many as possible. So after they were picked, we wrapped each one separately in newspaper and stacked them on wooden trays in the garage. We looked forward with anticipation to eating our own apples throughout the winter, but by Christmas they were all rotten. I spoke to a farmer friend about this and he said it was because I had picked them too soon. I protested that they looked ripe. Yes, he said, but did they come away easily? He explained that the right time to pick apples is when they come away from the branch easily into your hand. He told me that if you have to tug you should leave them because they are not ready for picking and will go rotten.

That was good advice on picking apples, but it is also good advice on dealing with the souls of men and women. This does not mean that we sit back and do nothing. If you

see souls that God seems to be awakening, then pray for
them, help them and advise them. But let the Holy Spirit
do his own special work, for only he can bring about the
new birth. When they have been made ready by the Spirit
of God, they will come easily and no pressure will be
needed. There are no rotten apples in a harvest that is
reaped by the Spirit.

Evidences of new life

When there is a genuine work of grace there will be
evidences of new life. These were lacking in Simon the
Sorcerer in Acts 8 but they were clearly seen in the
converts at Antioch in Acts 11. We are told that Barnabas
saw evidence of the grace of God. In Acts 11:19-30 five
aspects of this evidence can be found.

1. There was a great change in their lives

In Acts 11:23 Barnabas saw the grace of God evidenced
in people's lives. But grace is abstract and cannot be seen
or touched, so what did he see? You cannot see electricity,
but you can see the difference it makes when a light is
switched on in a dark room, and if you touch a bare wire
you will feel its power. So it is with the grace of God.
There was a difference in the people Barnabas met and a
power in their lives that had not been there before. 'If
anyone is in Christ', Paul tells the Corinthians, 'he is a
new creation; the old has gone, the new has come!' (2 Cor.
5:17).

When a man is converted certain things change. Some may happen immediately and some gradually, but either way there will be a change. It is bound to happen. John Newton continued in the slave trade for a time after he was saved but eventually fought for its abolition. Desires, ambitions and longings all change. Matthew Henry makes the point that if your 'salvation' has done nothing for your temper then clearly it has done nothing for your soul.

2. They loved the Lord Jesus Christ

In Acts 11:26 we read that the disciples were called Christians for the first time at Antioch. This was not a title they took upon themselves but was originally a name of scorn given to believers by the world. However, it demonstrates that unbelievers saw something in them, and heard things from them, that could only be explained by their new relationship to Christ. People who once worshipped idols with them, got drunk with them and cursed with them were now renouncing all these things and talking about their love for Christ. So they called them 'Christ-ians'. Love for Christ is a prime evidence of grace and if anyone does not evidence his new affection, we have no right to call him a Christian, whatever he professes to believe doctrinally. Of this love John writes, 'We love [him] because he first loved us' (1 John 4:19). Anyone who does not love Christ has not understood the love of Christ for sinners, and cannot therefore be a believer.

3. They loved the Word of God

These new believers were teachable and had a hunger for
Scripture. So they submitted themselves willingly to the
things taught by Paul and Barnabas. Spiritually newborn
babes 'crave pure spiritual milk, so that by it [they] may
grow up' (1 Peter 2:2), and this is a sure mark of grace.
Why should they have this desire? Because the Scriptures
testify to Christ and reveal him both in his glorious person
and his saving work. Those who love Christ will also love
his Word, the Bible.

4. They loved one another

The believers met together as a church, not because it was
a rule but a desire. All true Christians love fellowship in
the gospel with their fellow-believers (Phil. 1:5) and will
always seek it out. Notice also in Acts 11:29 the love they
had even for Christians they had never met. A new
convert does not have to be coaxed to go to church: he or
she longs to join with other believers in the worship of
God and the service of Christ.

5. They loved the lost

In Acts 11:24 we read that a great number believed and
came to Christ. This was after the initial blessing of verse
21, and came about through the ministry of Barnabas.
But it was also, no doubt, the result of the converts'
concern for others. The new Christians were not slow to
evangelize.

These, then, are some of the evidences of grace we need to look for when someone makes a profession of faith. But remember we are dealing with newborn babes and the evidence will not always be there in full maturity. When dealing with tender new life, we must guard against being naïve and gullible on one hand, and too critical on the other. It is fruit we want to see, not mere results. Results may bring praise to us but only fruit will bring glory to the Lord.

5.
Saviour and Lord

There are issues that we need to be clear about if our evangelism is to be effective. What are we actually trying to achieve in witnessing to unbelievers? How are we to present the gospel to them? What is the thinking that governs the unbelieving mind, and what do we expect from evangelism? Over the next four chapters we shall examine these questions by considering what our aim in evangelism should be. In this chapter we continue and extend the subject of the fruit of evangelism. What should we look for in those who are converted?

The biblical aim of evangelism is to bring sinners to know Jesus as Saviour and Lord. Sadly many Christians do not accept this and teach that to 'accept Jesus as Saviour' is enough. They argue against what they call 'lordship salvation' and say this amounts to salvation by works. For them salvation need not produce any change in a sinner's behaviour: it is simply a matter of believing the facts of the gospel.

Such teaching is wrong and will inevitably produce wrong methods of evangelism. An 'easy believism', which ignores the biblical demand for repentance and true faith, has been widespread for years amongst some evangelicals. A light, frothy, entertaining 'gospel' is set before men, and being saved becomes little more than taking out a spiritual insurance policy. Impressive results may be produced, in terms of numbers, but where is the spiritual fruit? A. W. Tozer was right when he said, 'The Lord will not save those whom he cannot command. He will not divide his offices. You cannot believe on a half-Christ. We take him for what he is — the anointed Saviour and Lord who is King of kings and Lord of all lords! He would not be who he is if he saved us and called us and chose us without the understanding that he can also guide and control our lives.'[1]

Lordship insisted upon

In Ephesians 4:17 Paul insists strongly upon certain standards of behaviour for the Christian: 'I tell you this, and insist on it in the Lord, that you must no longer live as the Gentiles do, in the futility of their thinking.' He is insisting that the lordship of Christ must be clearly seen in the day-to-day lives of all who call Jesus their Saviour.

In Philippians 2:11 the apostle reminds us that the day will come when every tongue will confess that Jesus Christ is Lord. But the Christian does that *now* and his confession is more than words, more than a mere response of the tongue. Jesus makes this point very clearly at the end of the Sermon on the Mount: 'Not everyone who says to me, "Lord, Lord," will enter the kingdom of heaven, but only he who does the will of my Father who is in heaven. Many will say to me on that day, "Lord, Lord, did we not prophesy in your name, and in your name drive out demons and perform many miracles?" Then I will tell them plainly, "I never knew you. Away from me, you evildoers!"' (Matt. 7:21-23).

What Jesus is saying is that his lordship in a believer's life is not a matter of words, but of submission and obedience to his will and commands. Dr Lloyd-Jones, in his two-volume exposition of the Sermon on the Mount, spends three chapters on these verses and the chapter titles he uses are very significant: 'False peace', 'Unconscious hypocrisy' and 'The signs of self-deception'. Here were people who genuinely thought they were Christians but they had a false peace. They were hypocrites but unconscious of this awful fact. They professed the right things but did not submit to the will of Christ's heavenly Father.

To say, 'Jesus is Lord,' is the most profound statement I can make. It means that I totally surrender my life to Jesus Christ and seek to be obedient to him in all things. That is not easy; indeed it is very costly. For a Jewish Christian in the first century it meant at least isolation from his family and excommunication from the synagogue. It could mean death to say that Christ, rather than Caesar, was Lord. It was costly then, and it still is today. The lordship of Christ can prevent a Christian taking certain jobs. To insist on Christian standards of truth and integrity, when the boss wants his employees to lie and cheat, can mean missing promotion or facing dismissal. That is the reality of the lordship of Christ, yet it is to this that every believer is called.

In Ephesians 4 Paul, in effect, tells his readers, 'You have made a profession of faith and say Jesus is your Saviour; well and good. Now let us see the evidence of this in your new life, your new behaviour, as you surrender to the lordship of Christ.' Note how strong Paul is on this. He does not put Christ's lordship before them as a suggestion to be considered, or an optional extra to be taken on board in a few years' time. He insists upon it now. And he does so for several good reasons which we shall now consider.

Christ is Lord because of who he is

On the Day of Pentecost, Peter proclaimed to the Jews that 'God has made this Jesus, whom you crucified, both Lord and Christ' (Acts 2:36). If God has made him Lord, then how can anyone say he is not Lord? Long before he came to earth, the Son of God had been 'appointed heir of all things', for by him all things were made. Christ is the creator and sustainer of all things, upholding them by his word of power, and is the express image of God's person. He has ascended to the right hand of the Majesty in heaven (Heb. 1:2-3). Well might he be called 'King of kings and Lord of lords' (Rev. 19:16). If this is the degree of eminence the Father has bestowed upon his Son, how can we hold Christ in any less esteem?

Christ is Lord because of the nature of salvation

Paul has spelt out very clearly what it means to be a
Christian in Ephesians 2. His statement is both clear and
thrilling. It tells us first of all what a non-Christian is (vv.
1-3). The sinfulness, hopelessness and helplessness of the
man without Christ are seen here in all their terrible
reality. He is dead in transgressions, controlled by Satan,
ruled by his sins and under the wrath of God. Next, in
verses 4-18, we see what the grace of God can accomplish
in and for the sinner. He is brought to life spiritually,
saved by grace, delivered through faith, transformed in
his behaviour and exalted with Christ. Finally, in verses
19-22 we see the saved sinner established on the foundation of Christ, incorporated into the church of God and
indwelt by the Holy Spirit. What he was, he no longer is.
The contrast between the last four verses of Ephesians 2
and the first three can only be the result of a creative and
transforming work of one who is Lord.

When a person is saved, he doesn't just kick the
gambling habit, stop getting drunk, and suchlike. Nor
does he merely become religious. Something tremendous
has taken place. There has been an explosion of grace in
his life and he is a new creation. Therefore he cannot live
as he once did. Why? Because he has a new Master, even
Christ. In other words, you cannot have Jesus as your
Saviour if he is not also your Lord. Or to put it more
theologically, justification and sanctification are closely
related to each other.

Justification is a once-and-for-all act of God whereby he declares the guilty sinner, now covered with the righteousness of Christ, accepted in his beloved Son. Because this is an act of God it is a perfect and finished work. There are no degrees of justification and so no Christian can ever be more justified than he is at the moment he is saved. The believer is also sanctified, or set apart, in Christ from the moment of conversion. Paul tells the Corinthians (who were far from perfect), 'You were washed, you were sanctified, you were justified in the name of the Lord Jesus Christ and by the Spirit of our God' (1 Cor. 6:11). He also tells them that Christ 'has become for us ... our righteousness, holiness [or "sanctification"] and redemption' (1 Cor. 1:30). These verses show that it is not possible to be justified without also being sanctified, that is, separated to the work of honouring God by our obedience to his Word. If Christ is our righteousness, he must also be our Lord.

There is also a sense in which sanctification can be regarded as a process in which we are called upon to co-operate with God, so that there are degrees of sanctification. We can grow in grace or we can backslide, and in this world of sin we shall never know perfect sanctification. This is why Paul needs to insist on the lordship of Christ in the Christian's life. He demands that we submit to God in obedience and delight, and thus advance and fulfil the work of sanctification. Paul is totally in agreement with James that 'Faith without works is dead' (James 2:20, NKJV).

Christ is Lord because he loved us

Jesus is the one who loved and died for us when we were
still his enemies (Rom. 5:8). Such a Saviour deserves our
obedience. Because he has already demonstrated the
greatness of his love, we can be sure that he will only
demand from us what is good for us. Thus the lordship of
Jesus is altogether logical. It is demanding, but it is
reasonable. The Bible says the commandments of the
Lord are 'not burdensome' (1 John 5:3) and Jesus tells us
that his yoke is easy and his burden light (Matt. 11:30).
These verses do not say that there are no commands to
obey and no yoke to bear, but they do say that, for the one
who loves the Lord Jesus Christ, obedience is a delight
and not a chore. Our Lord is no taskmaster who demands
the impossible, but a loving Saviour who, with every
command, supplies both the incentive and ability to obey.
It is altogether reasonable then that Paul should insist we
live our lives under the lordship of Jesus.

That is why he insists on Christ's lordship in our lives.
But what actually is he insisting upon in practical terms?
There is nothing vague about Paul's teaching on this
matter and in the remaining chapters of Ephesians he
explains what the lordship of Jesus means in the everyday
life of a believer. He does this first of all in principle and
then in practice.

The principle of a sanctified life

The principle is stated in Ephesians 4:22-24: 'Put off your old self ... and ... put on the new self.' The old self, or the old man, says Dr Lloyd-Jones, 'is what we are by birth and by nature: fallen, polluted, depraved, corrupt, sinful, with a bias against God and towards evil. Sin is universal. Therefore, says the apostle, I am telling you to put off that old man. Put him off!'[2] James Montgomery Boyce explains: 'The apostle is not merely urging a new and higher standard of morality on people. That is an utterly futile thing. We cannot be genuinely better by mere moral suasion. That is not it at all. Rather, Paul is demanding a high form of behaviour precisely because something decisive has already taken place. We have already been made new in Christ. That is why we should and must act like it.'[3] The principle is, 'You are new creations in Christ, so act that way!' Paul repeats this truth again in Ephesians 5:8: 'For you were once darkness, but now you are light in the Lord. Live as children of light.'

Paul's exhortation, 'Put off ... put on,' implies that a conscious effort is needed to change our lifestyle. It is not something that just happens, but has to be worked at. It is no use merely *wanting* to be a better Christian, or *wanting* to be more prayerful and more spiritual. You must *do* something about it. This is not salvation by works. Paul is not dealing here with our justification before God, but with the life of one who has already been justified. Salvation is all of grace, but that salvation has a purpose.

Paul spells this out in Ephesians 2:10: 'We are God's workmanship', says the apostle, emphasizing God's work of grace. But he continues, 'created in Christ Jesus to do good works, which God prepared in advance for us to do'. We were saved by grace so that we might serve by works. We were spiritually dead, but are now spiritually alive and true spiritual activity is possible. Not only is it possible, but God has ordained it to be our way of life if we truly are his children.

The practice of a sanctified life

The apostle then tells us in detail what it means in certain areas of our life to walk in good works. There will be no lies, either to the tax man or to the family (Eph. 4:25). Anger will be controlled (vv. 26-27). There will be no stealing, either from our employer or from the shops. We shall work if at all possible so as to have money to help others (v. 28). We shall be careful how we speak (v. 29) — and so Paul continues into chapter 5.

Some Christians, when confronted with such teaching, cry, 'That's legalism!' But that is not the case. Legalism is being enslaved by manmade rules. What we are considering here are the rules that God has made, not man. It is amazing how many sins in the lives of believers are excused by labelling the rules of God's Word 'legalistic'. Or we may be tempted to defend our disobedience by saying, 'The Lord has not convicted me of that.' But the Lord does not have to convict us if he has clearly commanded, and there is nothing clearer than the command of Scripture that we should live a Christlike life.

Evangelism involves telling sinners that they need to be saved from the consequences of their sin, but it must also tell them the consequences of salvation. Evangelism needs to be more interested in fruit than results, and the fruit we must look for is the beauty of Jesus exhibited in lives once fouled by sin. This is New Testament evangelism, to preach Jesus as Saviour and Lord.

6.
All things to all men

The biblical phrase 'all things to all men' has been used to justify all sorts of weird and wonderful innovations in church life and particularly in evangelism. 'Anything goes,' seems to have become the watchword in the last forty years, with 'Does it work?' as the only criterion. By 'work' is meant the production of instant numerical results. Probably the most extreme example of this kind of thinking was that of an American group that worked amongst students in the sixties. They encouraged their female members to have sex with male students to encourage them to come to their meetings. It could be argued that such an example is so extreme that it is totally irrelevant to most evangelical churches. That is probably true, but all action, whether moderate or extreme, is dictated by the principles we adopt. The idea that 'Anything is all right as long as it gets results,' is a basic error however it may be put into practice.

That being the case, it is important to understand what Paul meant when he wrote, 'I have become all things to all men so that by all possible means I might save some' (1 Cor. 9:22).

Rights and responsibilities

In 1 Corinthians 8 and 9 the apostle is dealing with the subject of rights and responsibilities. In chapter 8 the issue is one that was a very real problem in first-century churches, namely the consumption of food sacrificed to idols. The animals that people sacrificed to idols in the various pagan temples were often sold afterwards for food. Should Christians buy and eat such meat? Paul deals with this simply and clearly. We know, he says in verse 4, an idol is nothing and a non-existent god can in no way affect the meat. In other words, there is no problem, so go ahead and eat if you want to.

But 1 Corinthians 8:7 shows that not every believer knows and understands this. So, argues Paul in verse 9, be careful what you do in case you cause offence in this matter to weaker Christians who are sensitive about eating such meat. His conclusion in verse 13 is, 'Therefore, if what I eat causes my brother to fall into sin, I will never eat meat again, so that I will not cause him to fall.' Paul is saying, 'You have the right to eat this meat but you have also responsibilities to other believers and that means that you may have to forego your rights.'

In 1 Corinthians 9 the subject is different, but the principle is the same. The preacher has the God-given right to live off the gospel (v. 14). But at Corinth, because of certain problems in the church, Paul did not exercise this right (v. 15). He is arguing that in all his actions the believer should think of others, not himself. He sums up in chapter 10:23-24: '"Everything is permissible" — but not everything is beneficial. "Everything is permissible"

— but not everything is constructive. Nobody should seek his own good, but the good of others.'

At the end of chapter 9 he applies the same principle to the believer's attitude to unbelievers in evangelism. Imagine a Christian witnessing to a non-Christian. He wants to see that person come to faith in Christ, but how does he go about it? Paul's principle is that you take account of the unsaved person's outlook. You do not expect him to understand your way of thinking at once. You must remember who and what he is — his background, beliefs, attitudes — and you meet him at a level he can understand.

Paul cites in 1 Corinthians 9 the great privilege, for a first-century man, of being a citizen of Rome, and therefore being free and not a slave. The apostle was a Roman citizen but says that he would gladly forsake the rights and privileges of his citizenship, and make himself a slave, if this would help someone come to faith in Christ. He was willing to use every legitimate means to win the lost, regardless of the cost to himself. To the slave, he would become a slave, that he might thereby lead him to Christ. It is in this sense and in this context that he makes his statement about becoming 'all things to all men'.

Legitimate means are those that do not violate biblical principles. Clearly the use of sex to entice men to attend a meeting violates those principles. So too does co-operation in evangelism with men who deny the gospel, or watering down the gospel to make it more attractive to sinful people. All our methods must be subjected to the test of biblical legitimacy. But we must be careful to apply only biblical criteria. There may be ways and means of evangelism that are new to us, and differ from our past practices, but do not violate biblical principles. They may violate our traditional patterns and personal likes and dislikes, but do not offend biblical principles. If Paul was prepared to forego his rights and privileges to reach the lost sheep of Christ, then we ought also to lay aside our comfortable prejudices and be ready to use 'all means' to this same end. Such means, however, must pass the test that they are biblical, appropriate and applicable in a given situation.

A passionate obsession

From 1 Corinthians 9:19 to the end of the chapter it is not difficult to see that Paul had a passionate obsession to win souls. Five times he uses the verb 'to win', which implies striving, discipline and effort, before (in verse 22) he changes it to 'save'. At stake was not the success or failure of a methodology but man's eternal destiny. Paul *was* concerned with success in evangelism, but not to further his reputation as a preacher; rather, he longed to see souls saved. He also felt under a solemn obligation to share the gospel with all men. 'I am bound', he asserts, 'both to Greeks and non-Greeks, both to the wise and foolish. That is why I am so eager to preach the gospel also to you who are at Rome' (Rom. 1:14-15).

This is why he approached the task of evangelism with such passion and vigour. Do we? So often we evangelize because we feel we should and because we have to live up to our name as 'evangelicals'. It then becomes a mere duty, with the emphasis upon ourselves, not the unbeliever. Do we have the time? Can we fit it in? Will it be inconvenient? How much will it cost? We become more concerned with methods that suit us than with the lost souls of men and women. We are more concerned with our rights than our responsibilities. We become afraid that if we do something new or different we may violate the party line and bring the criticism of other churches upon ourselves.

Paul was prepared to break all his religious traditions in order to win those who were totally beyond the reach of normal religious connections. His God-given, passionate obsession compelled him to take seriously Christ's command, not only to preach the gospel, but by doing so to win souls and make disciples.

A flexible approach

From the examples given in 1 Corinthians 9:20-22 it is clear that Paul had an astonishing flexibility of mind. His concern was to discover the methods that combined the greatest integrity with the greatest impact. Consider just one of his examples: 'To the Jews I became like a Jew, to win the Jews.' Paul was brought up a Jew and had laboured under the spiritual delusions of Jewish legalistic religion. Having been delivered from that blindness, he can now sum up his attitude towards the law of Moses by stating categorically that 'Christ is the end of the law' in regard to saving righteousness (Rom. 10:4). In spite of this, however, for the sake of those who were still in bondage to the law, he was willing to conform himself to practices he had forsaken in order to win them. Examples of this are the circumcision of Timothy in Acts 16:1-3, and the vow he took in Cenchrea (Acts 18:18). Note how, immediately after taking this vow, he went to Ephesus and 'went into the synagogue and reasoned with the Jews' (Acts 18:19).

Paul vigorously opposed the Judaizers' claim (Acts 15:5) that circumcision was essential for salvation, and in Galatians he uses some of the strongest language in the New Testament as he battles against this heresy. The very heart of the gospel of grace was at stake and he would not budge an inch. Yet in Acts 16 the apostle circumcised Timothy, to avoid offending the Jews who lived in that area. Probably some Christians would have accused Paul of compromise but it was not compromise; Paul was simply being 'all things to all men'. To Paul it meant nothing in gospel terms whether Timothy was circumcised or not, but it was an issue for the unbelieving Jews he wanted to reach with the message of Christ. They would not have listened if Timothy, the son of a Jewish mother, had not been circumcised. So Timothy was circumcised by the apostle. It was quite another matter when Jews who professed to be Christians insisted that circumcision was essential to salvation. 'We did not give in to them for a moment, so that the truth of the gospel might remain with you' (Gal. 2:5).

Commenting on Paul's action, John Newton once said, 'Paul was a reed in non-essentials and an iron pillar in essentials.' John Stott writes, 'What was unnecessary for acceptance with God was advisable for acceptance by some human beings.'[1]

Paul's flexibility should encourage us to take a fresh look at some of our attitudes to evangelistic methods. There is no flexibility allowed in the message or content of the gospel, but the method of presenting the unchanging truth may (and must) change from situation to situation. For instance, to preach for forty minutes on a complicated doctrinal point in an old-folk's home at the end of the day in a warm, stuffy lounge is plainly ridiculous. You feel like telling such a preacher, 'Talk about Jesus simply and briefly before they go to sleep on you!'

The purpose of evangelism, whether from a pulpit or on a one-to-one basis, is to tell people the gospel in such a way that they can understand it, relate to it, see its application to themselves and believe it. Of course, they can do none of these things unless enlightened by the Holy Spirit, but we have our responsibilities too. We have to think more about our hearers and less about ourselves. What are they capable of understanding? At what level do I approach them? Is my language comprehensible to them? Are my illustrations appropriate? We want to win people, not alienate them. We can't expect people today, who have no biblical background, to listen to us in the way that people brought up to regular church attendance might have done fifty years ago. We have to accept people for what they are and witness to them accordingly.

In seeking to simplify our presentation of the message, the message itself must not be lost. Some modern

translations of the Bible work on the assumption that
people today do not understand concepts such as sin,
righteousness, atonement, grace and so on. So they simply omit such words, replacing them by others devoid of
theological content. Such an approach emasculates the
gospel. Without key concepts, such as grace and righteousness, the gospel simply disappears. Our task is not to
abandon these concepts, but to *explain* them in ways that
can be understood by our biblically illiterate hearers.

Times change and so too must methods. What worked
forty years ago will not necessarily work today. I remember as a teenager preaching in the back streets of my home
town. When we started the open-air meeting the ladies in
the street would bring out chairs and sit on the pavement
to listen. They would expect to be given a hymn sheet so
that they could join in the singing. But what would
happen in the same streets today? The curtains would be
drawn and the volume on the TV turned up to shut out the
intrusion. The people in those streets still need the gospel
but obviously the methods of yesteryear are not reaching
them.

Every Christian knows how difficult it is to get unbelievers to come to church today. Why is this? They feel
awkward in church, out of place and embarrassed. Some
of them feel as much out of place in a church as a Christian
would feel going into a strip club. We need to understand
this and try to help them. If that means changing things we
love and cherish, so be it. Is not this the principle Paul is
teaching of rights and responsibilities? What I as a
Christian like or dislike is nothing compared to the

importance of unbelievers hearing and believing the gospel. The message of the gospel cannot change, but evangelicals today need something of the flexibility of mind of the apostle Paul with regard to their evangelistic methods.

Evangelical Christians have always been highly critical of the authority which Roman Catholics give to tradition in their church life. But an inflexible attitude to things like music, instruments and orders of service is no better. We too are in danger of giving to traditional activities a biblical authority they do not deserve. Things which we accept today as normal in our church life, like hymns, organs and open-air preaching, were once frowned upon and vigorously opposed when they were introduced. Even the introduction of the Authorized Version of the Bible instead of the Geneva Bible met with opposition.

So the need for flexibility is nothing new in the church. Today many people will not come to our normal services; therefore we must consider other methods of bringing the gospel to them. 'All things to all men' demands that we do this. Bearing in mind that a legitimate method is one that does not violate biblical principles, here are a few suggestions that churches have tried and have found effective.

Guest meals: a harvest supper or New Year's dinner with invitations printed for Christians to give to their friends. The invitations should clearly state that an after-dinner speaker will talk on some aspect of the gospel.

Home Bible Studies: friends and neighbours are invited to a Christian's home for a group Bible study. This can either be led by the one in whose home the meeting is held or by the pastor or some other experienced believer.

A Christmas carol service held on 'neutral ground' in a local hall. This can be done attractively and the gospel clearly preached. A similar idea is to invite some qualified speaker to address, from a biblical perspective, a topic of current importance. There is no reason why the topic should not be controversial (for example, abortion, creation and evolution) provided the speaker is master of his subject and willing to handle hostile questions afterwards!

Men's nights: most of our churches are short of men but some unbelievers will attend a men's meal where a speaker can talk to them with a straight and uncompromising message.

Coffee mornings: in some areas there are sufficient numbers of non-working wives and retired people to allow viable morning meetings in believers' homes. Often those who attend belong to churches which do not preach the gospel, and their need is as great as that of the unchurched majority. Again, the main feature should be the preaching of Christ, but this can be done from an armchair in a relaxed environment.

These, and other such methods, are not a substitute for worship services, but simply an additional means of reaching out to people with the gospel. They all involve effort. The special meetings will need to be well advertised, especially by personal invitations, and their effect will depend upon believing prayer.

Fear

While many Christians recognize their failure in evangelism, they become very fearful at any talk of a new approach or new methods. They have seen the excesses in recent years and the way the essential message of the gospel has been watered down to accommodate the unbeliever. They fear that any new thinking will become the thin end of the wedge that will eventually change the message as well as the method of evangelism. This is understandable and one cannot but deplore the easy believism that has replaced the biblical call for repentance and faith in Christ alone. But our evangelism must not be dictated by fears.

Flexibility of method does not mean copying the world, with entertainment becoming the main element of evangelism. Evangelism starts with the essential fact that the biblical message cannot be changed. As soon as a method requires the message to be amended to achieve success, it should be dropped like a hot potato. Nothing, nothing, justifies tampering with the gospel as revealed in the person and work of the Lord Jesus Christ. What flexibility *does* mean is that we accept that society is very different from what it was fifty years ago. We must give more prayer and thought to how we should reach today's people with the gospel. 'All things to all men' is not an excuse for compromise but an expression of deep concern for the state of the lost. It is a concern that does not sit down and wait for sinners to come to us, but seeks to reach out to men and women where they are and as they are. Its only fear is of failing to fulfil the commission of Christ to go into all the world with the gospel — the fear of hearing friends and neighbours say, on the Day of Judgement, 'You never told me.'

7.
Barriers to belief

What prevents a person coming to faith in Christ? The prime reason given in Scripture is that 'the god of this age', that is Satan, has blinded people's minds so that they cannot believe (2 Cor. 4:4). We can react to this truth in several ways. We can throw up our hands in despair and say there is nothing we can do; or (citing the sovereignty of God) we can argue that God alone can save and that he will save in his time, so there is nothing we need to do. Both of these reactions leave us sitting in our evangelical armchairs feeling snug and comfortable. Meanwhile, millions go to hell without hearing the gospel because of our lack of urgency. A proper understanding of the sovereignty of God will drive us to action, as we shall see.

What we often fail to grasp is that the devil attacks the minds of Christians as well as those of unbelievers. There are two major barriers to the salvation of the lost: wrong thinking on the part of unbelievers, and wrong thinking on the part of believers. In this chapter we shall look at the barrier in the sinner's mind: his fallen nature, how he thinks and what he believes. In the next chapter we shall look at the barriers created by cold, formal, lifeless evangelicalism.

The barrier in the sinner's nature

Who are these people we want to win for Christ? What do we know about their souls that need saving? The Bible describes them very clearly: they are spiritually dead (Eph. 2:1,5). In evangelism we are called upon to present spiritual truths to men and women who are incapable of understanding these truths because the god of this age has blinded their minds. We are like Ezekiel as he stood in the valley of dry bones: 'Can these bones live?' (Ezek. 37:1-14). Written right across the situation is the word 'impossible'. Spurgeon was right when he said, 'No minister living can save a soul; nor can all of us together, nor all the saints on earth or in heaven, work regeneration in a single person. The whole business on our part is the height of absurdity.'[1] Then why try? There are three good and essential reasons.

Firstly, we ourselves were once spiritually dead and the 'impossible' happened to us. We were saved. So we know from our own experience that the impossible is in fact possible.

Secondly, we know why it is possible. It is God who saves. Let us look at the context of 2 Corinthians 4:4: 'The god of this age has blinded the minds of unbelievers, so that they cannot see the light of the gospel of the glory of Christ, who is the image of God. For we do not preach ourselves, but Jesus Christ as Lord, and ourselves as your servants for Jesus' sake. For God, who said, "Let light shine out of darkness," made his light shine in our hearts to give us the light of the knowledge of the glory of God in the face of Christ.' In these glorious verses Paul is telling us that the salvation of a soul is a creative act of God, a work analogous to the creation of the universe itself. God himself illuminates the darkened heart. He sheds into the soul the light, not of creation, but of his own glory, revealed in Jesus Christ. Thus God, in his sovereign power, breaks through the darkness of spiritual ignorance and death, making himself known to the sinner in regenerating power. That is how salvation happens, and why it is possible.

Thirdly, God has purposed to save 'a great multitude that no one could count' (Rev. 7:9). He chose them in Christ 'before the creation of the world' that they might be 'holy and blameless in his sight' (Eph. 1:4). Paul tells us in Romans 8:29-30 that God foreknew them, predestined them to be like Christ, justified them and glorified them. Although much of this is still future in human experience, it is already an accomplished fact as far as God is concerned. Far from making us lazy about evangelism, the certainty that the elect will be safely gathered in is a great incentive to evangelize. When Paul was having problems in Corinth, God encouraged him with the words: 'Do not be afraid; keep on speaking, do not be silent. For ... I have many people in this city' (Acts 18:9-10). The 'many people' referred to were the elect who were still waiting to hear the message of salvation in

Christ. They would do so only if Paul continued to preach boldly. It is God who saves, yes. But he has also chosen to use the vehicle of the gospel to accomplish salvation, and we have a key part in making this gospel known.

The opening three verses of Ephesians 2 describe for us the nature of man in sin, but this is not a popular viewpoint today. If we were to ask the average person, 'What is man?', we would probably get one of two answers. They would either say that man is an evolving creature and getting progressively better, so there is no real problem. Give him a couple of million years or so and everything will be fine. Or else we might be told that man is essentially good and only needs a little help and guidance.

Neither of these views needs God or the gospel. But man is neither an evolving creature nor essentially good. He is as described in Ephesians 2:1-3, dead in sins, under Satan's control, living out the sinful desires of the flesh and of the mind, and subject to the wrath of God. This description is the only one that squares with the facts of history and experience. Man's history is full of wars, killings, disputes, corruption, greed, idolatry and the like, and the twentieth century is no better. If anything it is worse than the previous centuries, not least because mankind has greater power to do evil than ever before. The 'evolving creature' and 'essentially good' scenarios cannot explain this. But the Bible's analysis does.

Man today is conditioned by the whole social and educational system to reject the biblical view of man and accept these other theories. It becomes inevitable, then, that if people think about salvation at all, they only think in terms of morality or religious observance. In other words, they turn to good works. This seems so reasonable and plausible. A man may see he has a problem with sin (or whatever else he may call it) and feel he must do something about it. He must change his ways, turn over a new leaf, pull himself together. This is the religion of the natural man, but it completely ignores the force and truth of Ephesians 2:1-3. Paul counters this whole outlook by declaring that salvation is not by works but by grace. But as long as man believes the optimistic theories of his own goodness he will never take grace seriously and will cling to good works as a means of salvation. It is an easier way than repentance, and makes the sinner feel good.

The sinner has a false view of himself but he also has a false view of God. We are told that over eighty per cent of our nation believe in God. But just what do they believe? To them God is little more than a religious Santa Claus who comes around now and again to hand out goodies. He has nothing to do with normal life. Therefore he is not taken seriously, and men lapse into a false optimism about the future. Because God is a harmless do-gooder, we shall all go to heaven. There is no judgement and no hell. So there is nothing to worry about.

The barrier in the sinner's mind

In my book *I will never become a Christian* I tried to analyse the thinking of the natural man under the following headings. The unbeliever says, 'I will never become a Christian' because:

1. All Christians are hypocrites;
2. To do so would be to commit intellectual suicide;
3. Christianity is just a crutch for those who cannot face up to reality;
4. There is nothing special about Christianity;
5. Christians cannot even agree amongst themselves;
6. A God of love could not possibly allow all the evil and suffering there is in the world;
7. Religion, including Christianity, has been responsible for a good deal of trouble in the world.

We are not going to deal with each of these objections here, but we need to bear in mind two things about them. Sometimes they are mindless excuses, only half thought out, but sometimes they are very real problems in a person's mind. Either way, they are not difficult to deal with if people are genuinely looking for answers. If they are not, and only want an argument, then you face the problem of 'pearls before swine'. Sinclair Ferguson comments on this verse in Matthew 7:6: 'One of the lessons we need to learn, therefore, is to live with the cost of our message being rejected. While that is heart-breaking, we are taught in Scripture that it will happen. Fore-warned is fore-armed. We are not taken by surprise by rejecters of the gospel. We do not mindlessly continue to offer Christ to people irrespective of their response.'[2]

That may not be easy to accept but clearly Jesus is preparing us for this possibility in Matthew 7:6 and also in other passages where he tells the disciples to shake from their feet the dust of a city which rejects the gospel. This does not encourage a complacent, 'I've told them the gospel so it is up to them.' But it does protect us from self-recrimination and from depression that might deter us from further evangelism.

Understanding the unbeliever's mind

We were all unbelievers once but we quickly forget what that was like. Add to that the fact that things have changed drastically in attitudes to Christianity over the past twenty years. We have moved from a general indifference to open hostility to the gospel. It has always been true that the devil blinds people's minds to the gospel, but the unbelievers of today are not those of twenty or thirty years ago. There is a difference. Then it was fairly normal to go to church; now it is not. We have seen that it can involve culture-shock for unbelievers to enter a church. They feel out of place, uncomfortable and awkward.

We have to remember also that modern man's mind is largely conditioned by the media, with very negative attitudes to the church. Silly vicars in TV plays or outrageous public statements from bishops do not give Christianity a good press. Coupled with this is the unscriptural, sentimental, almost humanistic trash that is frequently promulgated in the name of Christianity in religious broadcasts. All this is enough to put anyone off the gospel. Add to this Religious Education in schools, often taught by unbelievers and based on the premise that all religions are equally valid, and we see that the mind of modern man is conditioned to reject biblical Christianity.

What is the answer to all this? Clearly as Christians we are encouraged that salvation is 'of the Lord'. It is all of grace and there is no substitute in evangelism for the power of the Holy Spirit. But God works through us and our approach should be summed up in two words: love and reality.

People today don't trust others as they once did. They do not trust politicians. They do not trust business people or commercial advertising. They have become cynical and expect to be cheated, and react accordingly in their attitudes and relationships. They need to be weaned from their suspicion by seeing that we love them and care for them. Love has to be shown in all sorts of practical ways. You will never reach your neighbours with the gospel if the only time you speak to them is to invite them to church.

Is it not true that most believers have very few friends who are not Christians? There are several reasons for this. When we were saved we were changed and some unbelieving friends, not being able to understand this change, cut us off. We also, on our part, may have cut off unbelieving friends, because their habits and interests were inconsistent with following Christ. Clearly, believers are not to be 'of the world'. But we remain in the world, and to cut off all friendships with non-Christians is, in evangelistic terms, disastrous. If we are uncomfortable with them, they will feel uncomfortable with us, and there will be little possibility of influencing them. Love for the lost means involvement with them, though not of course with their sins.

Then there is reality. Non-Christians need to see that our faith is real and meaningful to us. They are watching us all the time and looking to see how we cope as Christians with things like sickness, death, frustration, disappointment and sorrow. It is no use telling someone how wonderful it is to be a Christian, what joy and peace and satisfaction you have in Christ, and then reacting as the world reacts when troubles come. A consistent Christian walk is a powerful aid to evangelism. Without reality in life, all our professions of faith in Christ will ring hollow. Paul tells Titus that believers should 'adorn the doctrine of God our Saviour in all things' (Titus 2:10, AV).

8.
Without a vision

We turn now to the wrong thinking of some believers that can create a barrier to evangelism. Let us look, firstly, at a well-known verse in Proverbs: 'Where there is no vision, the people perish: but he that keepeth the law, happy is he' (Prov. 29:18, AV). In the NIV the verse reads, 'Where there is no revelation, the people cast off restraint; but blessed is he who keeps the law.' No vision means no revelation, no ministry of the Word of God. The second part of the verse substantiates this: the opposite of 'no vision' is keeping the law of God, and the one who does so is happy, in contrast to those who 'perish' or 'cast off restraint'. The verse refers to a situation when there is no word from God to guide, to direct, to give hope, or to excite and challenge the soul.

Without the Bible and its teaching we would have no future hope and the grave would be the end. Philosophy bereft of Scripture makes this life the only reality and breeds materialism and selfishness. Without the Bible we have no absolute standards, no authority other than what self regards as right or wrong. Above all, without the Bible we would have no knowledge of God, who reveals

himself in Christ. The result of all this is that people
'perish'; they cast off restraint and reap the due consequences of their sin, both in this life and eternally. We see
this everywhere today: the cause and effect are clear.

We *do* have the Bible, of course, and in spite of
widespread apostasy there are many biblical preachers
who believe the truth and proclaim it week by week. So
why are the churches so weak and ineffective in their
influence on the life of the nation? There can be very little
argument: it is because, in most evangelical churches,
there is no vision. There may be 'revelation' in the sense
of Bible-based preaching, though even here we often
preach a dull, Christless message. We need a true vision
of Christ in his saving power and glory. 'We see Jesus',
says Hebrews, 'who was made a little lower than the
angels, now crowned with glory and honour because he
suffered death, so that by the grace of God he might taste
death for everyone [all the elect]' (Heb. 2:9). Without the
vision of Christ and him crucified, we shall not preach a
living gospel.

Furthermore, there is often no vision in the sense of a
belief in what God can and will do. Consequently there is
little enthusiasm, commitment or expectation. Without a
vision we merely repeat and react. We repeat what we
have done before, because we have a good memory of the
past but sadly no vision for the future. We react nega-
tively to change because we are suspicious and afraid of
anything we do not understand.

Many devout and sincere Christians are convinced
that we need nothing new in terms of our approach and
methods in the church. There is a tendency to make a

virtue out of our evangelistic failure. I know this is true because I have done it myself. We see that we are not reaching unbelievers while other churches are; they seem to get followers, but we do not. Why not? Because (we argue) we are faithful to the Scriptures and they are not. Unbelievers will not come to our church but seem to enjoy going to theirs, so there must be something wrong with their church. Obviously they are not as faithful to the Scriptures as we are.

This argument is not without justification. The amazing growth of the charismatic movement is an example, where great numbers flock to churches in search of dramatic religious experiences. But we must not justify failure by pleading faithfulness. Let us at least be honest with ourselves. Sometimes we explain the failure of our churches by blaming God. He is sovereign, so it must be his will not to bless us. The conclusion we draw is that our ineffectiveness is not our fault, and there is nothing we need or can do. Often we blame our failure on the world. We say people are so materialistic, so hard, so sinful, they do not want the gospel. But when was it any different? And does it ever dawn on us that when the world dismisses the church as old-fashioned and irrelevant, there might perhaps be an element of truth in their stricture?

We need to ask ourselves, why is it that so many believers have given up on personal evangelism? We can repeat and react, but without a vision it is impossible to respond to the spiritual needs of those around us. What happens when, in contrast to all this, the church *does* have an expectation of what God can and will do? To answer this let us look at two other passages of Scripture.

2 Kings 6:8-23

This passage presents a scene of seeming hopelessness
and imminent defeat. But in reality the situation was
never hopeless and there was no possibility of defeat.
Elisha knew this but his servant did not because he could
not see what the prophet saw.

The King of Aram was angry with Elisha and sent a
strong force of soldiers to capture him. They surrounded
the city where the prophet was staying and when Elisha's
servant saw them he was filled with dread and hopelessness. 'Oh, my lord, what shall we do?', he cried. Elisha's
calm reply was: 'Don't be afraid... Those who are with us
are more than those who are with them.' These were not
words of empty bravado, but a statement of spiritual
reality. They express what is true for all God's people at
all times, if we could only see it. The servant remained
blind to this reality until the prophet prayed, 'O Lord,
open his eyes so that he may see.' God answered the
prayer and the servant suddenly saw 'the hills full of
horses and chariots of fire all round Elisha'.

There is a sense of hopelessness about much of Christianity today. That is why Christians do not witness.
'What is the use?' they say. This is why Christians will
not attend prayer meetings. 'What is the point?' they ask.
Hopelessness thrives where there is no vision. Look again
at verse 16: 'Those who are with us are more than those
who are with them.' Do we believe that? Do we believe
that the resources of Christ exceed those of the devil? Do
we still believe in a sovereign God? If so, then let us use
this belief not to excuse failure but to assure us of victory.

Our prayer should be: 'Lord, put our thinking right and open our eyes to see your might and glory, for you are the one who works out everything in conformity with the purpose of your own will' (Eph. 1:11). It was because they had this confidence in the power of God that the early Christians 'preached the word wherever they went' in spite of the threat to their lives (Acts 8:4). If we have a clear view of the resources that are in Christ Jesus, we shall do the same. Jesus said, 'All authority in heaven and on earth has been given to me. Therefore go and make disciples of all nations' (Matt. 28:18-19). The authority and resources of Christ are the starting-point for evangelism.

John 4:35-38

A lack of vision frustrates evangelism. When the church is thus afflicted, it cannot see and appreciate the needs of people. We may occasionally pray, 'Lord, save souls', but we do nothing to win souls. Look at the words of Jesus in John 4:35: 'Do you not say, "Four months more and then the harvest"? I tell you, open your eyes and look at the fields! They are ripe for harvest.'

We should not think that perhaps we may see conversions next year or some time in the future. Jesus told his disciples to open their eyes and see both the present need and the present opportunity. Men and women need to be saved *now*, not at some unknown future date. The sinner's need never changes, but what must change is the Christian's appreciation of it. Do you see your town, spiritually speaking, as a wasteland or a harvest field? If the latter, are you prepared to get out into that field and work? If our eyes were opened to see what Jesus saw, if we really had a vision both of the need and of God's power to meet it, we would not be able to keep ourselves out of the harvest field.

Vision comes *via* revelation as God speaks to us through his Word. God always speaks, but we do not always listen. What is God saying to you in regard to evangelism? Is he saying, 'You are all right. Do nothing more. Be the same as you were last year and the year before. You do not need to change. All is well'? Or is he saying, 'Open your eyes, trust me, follow me, believe me. Work with me in the harvest field'?

9.
Gospel preaching

In this and the next two chapters we are going to consider the subject of gospel preaching. I realize that many who read this book will not be preachers, but these chapters are nevertheless relevant to all believers. Whether we are preachers or hearers, we need to re-examine what we expect from the ministry of the Word. What should we look for? What do we need to hear from the pulpits of our churches? True gospel preaching will not only fulfil the preacher's ministry, but will revive the desire of every believer to make Christ known.

Spurgeon said, 'Soul-winning is the chief business of the Christian minister.'[1] He did not say it is the *only* business of the minister, but that it is certainly the chief business. To dispute this would be to deny the whole thrust of the New Testament regarding the work of the church of Christ. For a preacher to neglect his chief business is a denial of his calling, yet many good biblical preachers openly admit that they feel more comfortable teaching saints than evangelizing sinners. And because there are few unconverted people attending their churches they have ceased preaching the gospel altogether.

If soul-winning is our chief business, and we are not winning souls, where does that leave our calling to preach? To quote Spurgeon again, 'Now, in the last place, the man whom Christ makes a fisher of men is successful. But, says one, "I have always heard that Christ's ministers are to be faithful, but that they cannot be sure of being successful." Yes, I have heard that saying, and one way I know it is true, but another way I have my doubts about it. He that is faithful is, in God's way and in God's judgement, successful, more or less. For instance, here is a brother who says that he is faithful. Of course, I must believe him, yet I never heard of a sinner being saved under him. Indeed, I should think, that the safest place for a person to be in if he did not want to be saved would be under this gentleman's ministry, because he does not preach anything that is likely to arouse, impress, or convince anybody ... he that never did get any fish is not a fisherman. He that never saved a sinner after years of work is not a minister of Christ. If the result of his life work is nil, he made a mistake when he undertook it.'[2]

Spurgeon preached that in 1886 just a few years before he died. It is not, therefore, the intolerant judgement of a young man, but the mature conclusion of an old one. To those of us who may go several years without seeing a conversion, it can sound daunting and devastating. Was Spurgeon revealing an unfair lack of sympathy with preachers less able than himself? It is not my business to defend the renowned Baptist, but I would urge all preachers to seek the answer in his book *The Soul Winner*. In the next two chapters I shall use several quotes from this book, because I believe it will help us to understand and share his thinking.

What is the real winning of a soul for God?

Spurgeon asks this question and then proceeds to answer it. He says first of all that the sinner must be instructed so that he may know the truth of God. He cites Matthew 28:19-20: 'Go ... and teach all nations ... teaching them to observe all things whatsoever I have commanded you,' (AV) and concludes that *teaching* is the heart of gospel preaching. All too often we seem to accept as a fact that there will be less content in a sermon for sinners than a sermon for saints. Spurgeon would strongly disagree with that. He argues that the gospel is good news and that 'There is information in it, there is instruction in it concerning matters which men need to know, and statements in it calculated to bless those who hear it. It is not a magical incantation, or a charm, whose force consists in a collection of sounds; it is a revelation of facts and truths which require knowledge and belief. The gospel is a reasonable system, and it appeals to men's understanding; it is a matter for thought and consideration, and it appeals to the conscience and the reflecting powers.'[3]

This point is emphasized by Paul's example at the jail at Philippi. The great question is asked: 'What must I do to be saved?' The answer is given: 'Believe in the Lord Jesus, and you will be saved.' But Paul did not leave it at that. What exactly was the jailer to believe? Who was

Jesus Christ? Acts 16:32 is crucial: 'Then they spoke the word of the Lord to him and to all the others in his house.' It was as a result of *that* preaching of the gospel that the jailer and his family were saved. Spurgeon goes on: 'And, do not believe, dear friends, that when you go into special evangelistic services, you are to leave out the doctrines of the gospel; for you ought then to proclaim the doctrines of grace rather more than less. Teach gospel doctrines clearly, affectionately, simply, and plainly, and especially those truths which have a present and practical bearing upon man's condition and God's grace. Some enthusiasts would seem to have imbibed the notion that, as soon as a minister addresses the unconverted, he should deliberately contradict his usual doctrinal discourses, because it is supposed that there will be no conversions if he preaches the whole counsel of God. It just comes to this, brethren: it is supposed that we are to conceal truth and utter a half falsehood, in order to save souls... This is a strange theory and yet many endorse it. According to them, we may preach the redemption of a chosen number to God's people, but universal redemption must be our doctrine when we speak with the outside world; we are to tell believers that salvation is all of grace, but sinners are to be spoken with as if they were to save themselves... We have not so learned Christ. He who sent us to win souls neither permits us to invent falsehoods, nor to suppress truth. His work can be done without such suspicious methods.'[4]

John Elias makes the same point: 'There is a great defect in the manner of many preachers. It can scarcely be said that the gospel is preached by them... Though these preachers may not be accused of saying what is false, yet, alas, they neglect stating weighty and necessary truths when opportunities offer. By omitting these important portions of truth in their natural connection, the Word is made subservient to subjects never intended. The hearers are led to deny the truth which the preacher leaves out of his sermons. Omitting any truth intentionally in a sermon leads to the denial of it.'[5]

Spurgeon and Elias were soul-winners so we must listen to them. They were not advocating heavy theological sermons that the unconverted will not be able to understand: they were stressing the need to preach the full gospel. If sinners are to be saved they must hear the truth, and all the truth. It is our failure at this point that produces the sort of wishy-washy conversions that give churches so many pastoral problems. We owe it to men and women to tell them all the gospel — to speak of God's eternal purposes in Christ, of election, calling, justification and redemption; of both God's love and wrath; of both heaven and hell; of both grace and human responsibility. Spurgeon says, 'The preacher's work is to throw sinners down in utter helplessness, that they may be compelled to look up to him who alone can help them. To try to win a soul for Christ by keeping that soul in ignorance of any truth, is contrary to the mind of the Spirit... The best attraction is the gospel in all its purity. The weapon with which the Lord conquers men is the truth as it is in Jesus. The gospel will be found equal to every emergency; an arrow which can pierce the hardest heart, a balm which will heal the deadliest wound. Preach it, and preach nothing else.'[6]

Spurgeon's second answer to the question: 'What is the real winning of a soul?' is that we need to impress the sinner so that he feels his need of Christ. In this he keeps the balance between content and presentation. He says, 'A purely didactic [teaching] ministry, which should always appeal to the understanding, and should leave the emotions untouched, would certainly be a limping ministry.'[7] He then proceeds to make the powerful statement that 'A sinner has a heart as well as a head; a sinner has emotions as well as thoughts; and we must appeal to both. A sinner will never be converted until his emotions are stirred.'[8]

For most of us who love the Bible, it is relatively easy to preach the truth and give a faithful exposition of Scripture. The difficult thing is to preach the truth in such a way that we stir the hearts and prick the consciences of sinners. An easy way out is to say that only the Holy Spirit can do this. That is true, but is it the whole truth? We must not use this as an excuse to avoid our responsibilities and reduce preaching to mere lecturing.

How can we preach so that sinners' hearts are stirred? It is not by filling the sermon with sentimental stories and heart-rending illustrations. That may well stir emotions but it will not lead to salvation. That is the method of the actor, not the preacher. Neither will we succeed by filling the service with gimmicks and working up an atmosphere. So how do we do it? We do it in three ways.

Firstly, by having regard to *the content of our message*. What should that content be? We preach, said Paul, 'the unsearchable riches of Christ' (Eph. 3:8). If Christ is not the heart of every sermon, then these riches will be missing and our hearers will go away impoverished. We may use the Bible to preach morality, judgement, history, ecclesiology, eschatology, and so much else. But unless we unveil Christ 'in all the Scriptures' (Luke 24:27) we shall leave men forlorn and shut the door to grace.

Secondly, we shall affect our hearers by *preaching to them and for them*. This means plenty of application all the way through the sermon, pointing the truths, pushing them home, and showing their relevance to the everyday affairs of life. In this way we will guard against being heavy and boring. Sadly, according to many of God's people who listen to sermons every week, a lot of preachers are simply dull. Their content may well be biblical, but their presentation is so dry that their hearers soon 'switch off'. Our application of Scripture truth must be such that every sinner who hears us knows that God is speaking about, and to, him or her. Sinners are great wrigglers and they must not be allowed to wriggle out of conviction of sin. Furthermore, our application must be appropriate. For instance, if we go on and on about AIDS, the vast majority of unregenerate men and women in the congregation will totally agree. They will be comfortable, even enjoying our tirade, because we are preaching about a sin of which they are not guilty. We must point up the ordinary sins of ordinary people.

We should not confuse application with illustration. A well-chosen illustration can help enormously in bringing home a point, and in lightening our presentation. But some preachers go overboard in their attempt to be interesting. Illustrations should be neither too lengthy nor so frequent that they destroy the train of thought and logic. If they are to listen well, people must be able to follow the preacher's argument and line of reasoning.

Thirdly, we must give attention to the *manner* in which we preach. Richard Baxter said, 'I preached as never sure to preach again, and as a dying man to dying men.'[9] In other words, he had a sense of urgency, of deep concern, of warmth and passion. Speaking of pathos, Dr Martyn Lloyd-Jones said, 'A special word must be given also to the element of pathos. If I had to plead guilty of one thing more than any other I would have to confess that this perhaps is what has been most lacking in my own ministry. This should arise partly from a love for the people. Richard Cecil, an Anglican preacher in London towards the end of the eighteenth century and the beginning of the nineteenth, said something which should make us all think: "To love to preach is one thing; to love those to whom we preach is quite another." The trouble with some of us is that we love preaching, but we are not always careful to make sure that we love the people to whom we are actually preaching. If you lack this element of compassion for the people you will also lack the pathos which is a very vital element in all true preaching.'[10]

If we do not feel for the people, and do not feel the power and significance of what we are preaching, they will never feel their need of the gospel. It will come across to them as mere words and nothing more. The gospel has to grip our hearts both in our preparation and in the pulpit. It ought to excite us and this will be conveyed to our hearers. Are we afraid of emotion in the pulpit? Lloyd-Jones, having distinguished between emotion and emotionalism, complains, 'Emotion is regarded as something almost indecent. My reply to all that, once more, is simply to say that if you contemplate these glorious truths that are committed to our charge as preachers without being moved by them there is something defective in your spiritual eyesight.'[11]

We are not to preach as lecturers, detached from their subject. Neither are we to preach with the silly excitement of actors doing a TV commercial. Our business, according to Spurgeon, is to 'continue to drive at men's hearts till they are broken; and then we must keep on preaching Christ crucified till their hearts are bound up; and when that is accomplished, we must continue to proclaim the gospel till their whole nature is brought into subjection to the gospel of Christ.'[12]

The preaching we need today

In his biography of Jonathan Edwards, Iain Murray has a remarkable chapter entitled 'The Breaking of the Spirit of Slumber'. In this he deals with the type of preaching needed in the 1730s because of the spiritual condition of the day. He says, 'It has sometimes been assumed that the preaching of the eighteenth century leaders in the revivals in North America was simply continuing a well established tradition. That, however, is not the case. The commonly accepted preaching was not calculated to break through the prevailing formalism and indifference, and the preaching which did bring men to a sense of need and humiliation before God was of a very different order.'[13]

What was this different preaching that God so richly blessed? Edwards said, 'I know it has long been fashionable to despise a very earnest and pathetical way of preaching, and they only have been valued as preachers who have shown the greatest extent of learning, strength of reason, and correctness of method and language. But ... an increase in speculative knowledge in divinity is not what is so much needed by our people as something else. Men may abound in this sort of light, and have no heat... Our people do not so much need to have their heads stored as to have their hearts touched, and they stand in the greatest need of that sort of preaching which has the greatest tendency to do this.'[14]

We are facing people today, in and out of the church, who have little sense of the evil of sin and little love for God. Preaching that merely fills their heads with facts but does not touch their hearts is not going to change anything. Edwards described the people of his day as 'stupidly senseless to the importance of eternal things'.[15] Therefore they needed preaching which would ensure that 'their conscience stares them in the face and they begin to see their need of a priest and a sacrifice'.[16] Note the emphasis on Christ. Such preaching starts with the preacher's apprehension of Christ in his glorious person and saving power. It continues as he feels the urgency of the task and is satisfied with nothing less than the glory of God in the salvation of sinners. Finally, it requires an experience of, and dependence on, the Holy Spirit, who will honour a Christ-centred ministry. Iain Murray says, 'True heart-searching, humbling and convicting preaching requires an experimental acquaintance with the Spirit of God on the part of the preacher.'[17]

Murray concludes the chapter with these words: 'The preaching through which the spirit of slumber was broken in the 1730s was searching and convincing. A band of men was being raised up for whom the gravity of sin, the possibility of an unsound profession of Christ, and the carelessness of a lost world were pressing burdens. Behind their public utterances was their vision of God and of eternity.'[18]

10.
The gospel preacher

If souls are to be saved it will be by the sovereign will of God, but preachers of the gospel are a key factor in the working out of God's will. It is true that God overrules our inadequate preparation, prayerlessness and sin, but that does not relieve us of the responsibility of being and doing what the Lord requires of us. So we need to ask, what sort of man should the preacher of the gospel be?

The preacher and God

There is nothing more important for us than our relationship with God — in other words, personal holiness. It is not difficult to prepare a faithful exposition of Scripture and to preach a good sermon. Professionalism and experience can handle that. But to preach sermons whose end result will be the salvation of souls takes more than this. It takes a man who has been in the presence of God, who has been instructed by God, who knows something of the mind of God and who feels for souls in some measure as

God does. It takes holiness, and no amount of professionalism and experience can produce that.

Holiness is not sinlessness. That is not possible in this
life. Holiness involves a hatred of all known personal sin
and a longing to know God in a deeper and more intimate
way. For the holy man, sin is the greatest burden, a source
of sorrow and trouble. And his greatest longing is for God
himself. Holiness in the preacher will produce such a
desire to be at one with God that, when he preaches, the
Word of God will come undistorted by human sin.
Spurgeon urges preachers: 'Dear brethren, I do beg you
to attach the highest importance to your own personal
holiness. Do live unto God. If you do not, your Lord will
not be with you... You may preach very fine sermons, but
if you are not yourselves holy, there will be no souls
saved. The probability is that you will not come to the
conclusion that your lack of holiness is the reason for your
non-success; you will blame the people, you will blame
the age in which you live, you will blame anything except
yourself; but there will be the root of the whole mischief.'[1]

Notice how Spurgeon analyses the effects of unholi-
ness in the preacher: 'You will blame the people.' Is that
what we do? Hudson Taylor makes the same point:
'Perhaps if there were more of that intense distress for
souls that leads to tears, we should more frequently see
the results we desire. Sometimes it may be that while we
are complaining of the hardness of the hearts of those we
are seeking to benefit, the hardness of our own hearts and
our own feeble apprehension of the solemn reality of eternal things may be the true cause of our lack of success.'[2]

Andrew Bonar says of Robert Murray M'Cheyne, 'He entertained so full a persuasion that a faithful minister has every reason to expect to see souls converted under him, that when this was withheld, he began to fear that some hidden evil was provoking the Lord and grieving the Spirit. And ought it not to be so with all of us? Ought we not to suspect, either that we are not living near to God, or that our message is not a true transcript of the glad tidings, in both matter and manner, when we see no souls brought to Jesus?'[3]

Bonar continues, 'Two things he seems never to have ceased from — the cultivation of personal holiness and the most anxious efforts to win souls.'[4] How M'Cheyne links these two things is highly significant. He wrote to William Burns in September 1840, 'I am also deepened in my conviction, that if we are to be instruments in such a work, we must be purified from all filthiness of the flesh and spirit. Oh, cry for personal holiness, constant nearness to God, by the blood of the Lamb. Bask in his beams — lie back in the arms of love — be filled with his Spirit — or all success in the ministry will only be to your own everlasting confusion... How much more useful might we be, if we were only more free from pride, self conceit, personal vanity, or some secret sin that our heart knows. Oh! hateful sins, that destroy our peace and ruin souls.'[5]

M'Cheyne believed that 'In the case of a faithful ministry, success is the rule and the lack of it the exception.'[6] And when there was no success, no souls saved, he did not blame the people but looked first at his own heart. We tend to think of M'Cheyne in terms of his holiness and saintliness, and quite rightly so. But holiness did not just happen to him; he cultivated it. This he did by a regular examination of his own heart and life. This examination he called 'reformation'. It is a very sobering experience to read about this in his memoirs. It was not morbid introspection, but the soul-searching of a minister of Christ longing to be more like his Master. Only thus, he believed, would he be usable in the salvation of the lost.

The preacher and himself

There are several things we need to consider under this heading, but they can all be summed up by the word 'confidence'.

Confidence in our call to preach the gospel

Without this confidence we shall never preach with courage and conviction. Without this confidence, the devil will walk all over us. During difficult times, when there is little success, and when conversions are few and far between, the only thing that keeps us going is the conviction that God has called us to preach. Every preacher at some time or other knows hard times. We wonder what we are doing in the ministry and the devil tempts us to give it all up. But the call remains unchanged and this is our anchor.

Confidence in the gospel

To the apostle Paul the gospel of 'the grace of Christ' was not merely a tool to be used or a method to follow. It was

everything. There was no alternative to it (Gal. 1:6-9); it
is more than sufficient for the fulfilment of God's purposes (Rom. 1:16). Most evangelicals will agree with
these sentiments in theory, but do we embrace them in
practice? To the early Christians there was no difference
between theory and practice. This meant they did not see
the need to prop up the gospel with current popular fads.
Neither did they apologize for the gospel, or feel embarrassed by certain aspects of it. They just preached it and
God blessed it. Confidence in the gospel really means
confidence in God and in Christ, for it is 'the gospel of
God ... regarding his Son' (Rom. 1:1-3). If we remember
this we shall be able to withstand the pressures put upon
us to water down the message.

What are these pressures? There are the intellectual
pressures that challenge us with questions over creation
and biblical inerrancy. Evangelicals are not as strong on
these issues as they once were and the temptation is ever
present for us to modify the truth to placate men. Is the
Bible inerrant or not? How we answer that question will
sooner or later determine how we preach the gospel.

There are also popular pressures put upon the preacher,
consciously or unconsciously, by Christians in the churches.
So very few unbelievers attend our services that Christians
sometimes want both Sunday services to provide teaching
for the saints. Thus pressure comes upon the preacher not to
preach the gospel. Or he may say, 'We do not have a gospel
service as such but I include a little of the gospel in every
sermon.' It is true that there should be enough gospel in every
sermon to save a soul but we also need sermons that are full
of the gospel — sermons whose sole aim is to save sinners.

Even if our congregations consist only of believers we still need gospel sermons. Surely there is no greater blessing for a Christian than to hear the gospel preached in the power of the Holy Spirit. And if we are careful to preach Christ, then gospel and instruction for believers will blend into a seamless whole. Sermons with a 'little of the gospel' in them are not enough. Spurgeon said, 'What you must do with your sermons is to make them red hot; never mind if men say you are too enthusiastic or even too fanatical, give them red-hot shot; there is nothing else half as good for the purpose you have in view. We do not go snow-balling on Sundays, we go fire-balling; we ought to hurl grenades into the enemy's ranks.'[7]

This leads us to another aspect of these popular pressures, namely people in the church who criticize gospel preaching that is too straight and clear for them. They particularly resent preaching on judgement and hell. The pressure this criticism puts upon the preacher is enormous. It is, of course, possible to preach too harshly or without love, and if this occurs criticism is warranted. But to leave out the harsher sounds of the gospel, and say nothing of the 'terror of the Lord' (2 Cor. 5:11, NKJV), is a rejection of the gospel itself. Only a confidence in the gospel as the Word of God will enable us to resist this pressure.

Confidence in preaching

Many evangelicals today have lost confidence in preaching. We may lament this and mourn the fact that in some

churches music and drama have replaced preaching. But
why has it happened? Is it not the fault of preachers
themselves? Is it not because gospel preaching too often
lacks authority, relevance and power, and consequently
fails to save souls? Dr Lloyd-Jones once said, 'The most
urgent need in the Christian church today is true preaching.'[8] Most preachers would agree with that but many
Christians in the pew do not. That is not surprising if the
preaching they hear is so sentimental as to have no substance, or so intellectual that they cannot comprehend it.

What is true preaching? What constitutes true gospel
preaching? It involves both a proper content and a correct
presentation. We have considered the content of the
gospel earlier, in some detail. What can we say of presentation? The gospel must be preached in a language that
people can understand. In the last century Spurgeon was
pleading, 'We need in the ministry, now and in all time,
men of plain speech. The preacher's language must not be
that of the classroom, but of all classes; not of the
university, but of the universe... "I use market language,"
said George Whitefield, and we know the result. We need
men who not only speak so that they can be understood,
but so that they cannot be misunderstood.'[9] In these days
of mass communication things may be different to some
extent. The problem no longer lies so much with words,
as with concepts and ideas. Plain speech is not slang but
simple language and concepts that people can understand.

When we stand before a congregation to preach the
gospel we must have two prime concerns: firstly, that the
Lord will be glorified; and secondly, that the people
before us will benefit from the preaching. The first can

hardly be fulfilled without the second. These concerns will govern the content, structure, length and presentation of the sermon. It is very easy to indulge our intellectual pretensions in the pulpit and think that the sole object of the exercise is that the people should hear us. The real object is that they should be saved and blessed by God.

True gospel preaching will aim at, and expect, conversions. A young preacher complained to Spurgeon that he saw no conversions. The great man answered, 'Do you expect the Lord to save souls every time you open your mouth?' 'No, sir', he replied. 'Well then,' said Spurgeon, 'that is why you do not get souls saved.' Now notice how Spurgeon applied that story: 'I had caught him very nicely; but many others would have answered me in just the same way as he did. They tremblingly believed that it is possible, by some strange mysterious method, that once in a hundred sermons God might win a quarter of a soul. They have hardly enough faith to keep them standing upright in their boots; how can they expect God to bless them? I like to go to the pulpit feeling, "This is God's Word that I am going to deliver in his name; it cannot return to him void; I have asked his blessing upon it, and he is bound to give it, and his purposes will be answered, whether my message is a savour of life unto life, or of death unto death to those who hear it."' [10]

We could dismiss all this by saying Spurgeon was an exception and his days were different from ours. There is some truth in that. But surely we believe that the gospel is *meant* by God to save souls and it therefore *ought* to save souls. Is it that we are afraid of this word 'success' in connection with gospel preaching, as if it is not spiritual to expect results? Spurgeon and M'Cheyne would not agree with that. Neither would Richard Baxter, who once said, 'Moreover, if you would prosper in your work be sure to keep up earnest desires and expectations of success. God seldom blesseth any man's work so much, as his whose heart is set on success. Let all that preach Christ and man's salvation be unsatisfied till they have the things they preach for.'

The preacher and the people

We have seen the need for love and pathos in preaching, and it is these that bring to preaching what Lloyd-Jones calls a 'melting quality'. This is a powerful and vivid phrase, describing something that all preachers should long for in their ministry. It is easy to be too harsh in gospel preaching, delighting to tell people that they are sinners and going to hell. Oh, to be able to preach of sin and hell with this melting quality! The only way to achieve this is to turn these awful doctrines into signposts to Christ. The law, says Paul, was 'put in charge to lead us to Christ, that we might be justified by faith' (Gal. 3:24). We must also love the people and really long for their salvation.

I wonder sometimes if this lack of love for sinners in our preaching is because we are not sure that God loves them. Is our love greater than God's, that we can love those he does not love? When some Christians argue, as they do most strongly, that God's love is for his elect and them alone and therefore a free offer of the gospel should not be made to all sinners, they are not propagating Calvinism but hyper-Calvinism. Calvinistic preachers like Whitefield, Spurgeon and Lloyd-Jones would all agree with John Calvin's comment on John 3:16: 'Although there is nothing in the world deserving God's favour, he nevertheless shows he is favourable to the whole world when he calls all without exception to faith in Christ.'[11] In John 3:16 there are two big, all-embracing words, 'whoever' and 'world'. We have seen Calvin's interpretation of the word 'world'; now here is his comment on 'whosoever': 'He has employed the universal term whosoever, both to invite all indiscriminately to partake of life, and to cut off every excuse from unbelievers.'[12]

In his book *Discourses and Sayings of our Lord,* John Brown argues: 'The revelation of mercy made in the gospel refers to men as sinners, not as elect sinners! The invitations and promises of the gospel calling upon men to believe in Jesus are addressed to all, and are true and applicable to all without exception... I am persuaded that the doctrine of personal election is very plainly taught in Scripture, but I am equally persuaded that the minister misunderstands that doctrine who finds it, in the least degree, hampering him in presenting a full and free salvation as the gift of God to every one who hears the gospel.'[13]

No gospel preacher need have any reservations in his mind when he stands before sinners. In the gospel, God is addressing every man, woman and child. God loves them and we are to love them and tell them, with pleadings and compassion, that they must come in repentance and faith to Jesus Christ.

11.
Evangelism and the law of God

To evangelize is to make known to sinners the good news of the gospel. It is to tell them that God so loved the world that he gave his only Son to die upon the cross, that those who believe in him should not perish for their sins, but instead receive everlasting life (John 3:16). Gospel preaching properly focuses upon the death and resurrection of Christ, because without these there is no atonement for sin, no justification, and thus no gospel. It was the love of God that made the cross possible. But it is the holiness of God that makes the cross necessary. If God were not holy he could treat sin as casually as we do, but his holiness demands that sin be punished legally and fully. The character of God demands that he must be just as well as the justifier (that is, the one who justifies the ungodly).

The law that God gave to Israel at Sinai, by the hand of Moses, is a verbal expression of the holiness of his character. It puts into words what God is, and what God expects. Thus when the law says, 'You shall have no gods beside me,' it is not evidence of petty resentment on the part of God, but of holy jealousy. God demands our sole obedience because all other gods are false gods and will lead us astray. The law, then, is restrictive only in order to be protective. It is for our good, or to put it another way, it expresses both God's holiness and his love. It is impossible to preach a full gospel without both these ingredients being present!

The aim of evangelism is to bring sinners to a saving experience of Christ. But how are sinners saved? The answer to that will determine whether or not there is any relationship between evangelism and law. If salvation is only a decision that the sinner makes in response to the offer of salvation; if it is simply 'deciding to accept Jesus as my Saviour', or merely 'giving my heart to Jesus' — then there will be no place for preaching the law, because there will be no place for either conviction of sin or repentance. Much of modern evangelism has bypassed the call for repentance because it has reduced salvation to an act of human will. It couches the offer of the gospel in language such as, 'To be happy you need Jesus'; 'You need Jesus to mend your marriage', and so on. In such 'preaching' the law of God would be an inappropriate intrusion.

But if salvation is impossible without conviction of sin and repentance, then the law is crucial. For it is the very purpose of the law to convince us of our sin, and only such conviction leads to repentance.

What is conviction of sin?

It is not 'conviction of sin' for a man to feel bad because he is drinking too much or generally making a mess of his

life. Sin is not just a violation of socially accepted
standards. To see sin only in social or moral terms will not
lead people to conviction. Sin must be seen in the light of
the law and holiness of God. The gospel is not an aspirin
for the aches of life, to soothe and comfort man in his
misery. It is a holy God's answer to the violation of divine
law by human beings whose very nature is to rebel against
him. So, says Dr Jim Packer, we are not preaching the
gospel, 'if all we do is to present Christ in terms of a man's
felt wants. (Are you happy? Are you satisfied? Do you
want peace of mind? Do you feel you have failed? Are
you fed up with yourself? Do you want a friend? Then
come to Christ...) ... To be convicted of sin means ... to
realize that one has offended God, and flouted his authority, and defied him, and gone against him, and put oneself
in the wrong with him. To preach Christ means to set him
forth as the one who through his Cross sets men right with
God again. To put faith in Christ means relying on him,
and him alone, to restore us to God's fellowship and
favour.'[1]

Most people think salvation is the product of morality
and religious observance. In spite of the clarity of the
New Testament message, they still cling to their own
efforts to save themselves. But salvation by works never
creates conviction of sin because it fails miserably to take
into account the holiness, purity and justice of God. It sees
sin only as a moral or social blemish and not as an affront
to the Word, law and character of God. It is the law of God
which produces conviction because it shows us our sin in
relationship, not to society and people, but to God. It
shows us that we have failed to meet God's requirements.

Salvation remains impossible as long as God's demands remain unsatisfied. What are God's demands? God requires from us a righteousness equal to his own. We may think that is unreasonable, but it is not. God created man sinless, and he wants us to be the way he intended us to be.

That is not unreasonable but it is impossible! Our sin makes it impossible. We cannot satisfy God's reasonable demands. So where does that leave us? It leaves us unable to save ourselves and needing a Saviour. And this Saviour will have to provide for us a righteousness as good as God's. Where can such a righteousness be found? In Christ, says the Bible. 'God made him [Christ], who had no sin, to be sin for us, so that in him we might become the righteousness of God' (2 Cor. 5:21). And it is this righteousness, Christ's own perfect righteousness imputed to the sinner, that is revealed in the gospel. 'I am not ashamed of the gospel, because it is the power of God for the salvation of every one who believes... For in the gospel a righteousness from God is revealed...' (Rom. 1:17). Thus the gospel makes known to us God's solution to the problem: in Christ, God provides for us the very righteousness that he demands. That is the gospel. There is a righteousness from God that comes to us through faith in Jesus Christ.

A sinner can hear all this and not make head or tail of it unless he is convinced of sin, unless he first sees his own helplessness and hopelessness. He must see that he is not meeting God's demands and that he can never meet them. He must see his sin in relationship to God and the function of the law is to show him just that. The law makes no attempt to compare one man with another; it takes us all to the yardstick of the holiness of God and there we all fail miserably.

The purpose of the law

Writing to the Galatians, Paul asks, 'What, then, was the purpose of the law?' (Gal. 3:19). A few verses later, he answers his own question: 'The law was our tutor to bring us to Christ' (Gal. 3:24). This is the role of the law in evangelism.

When we are talking of evangelism and the law of God it is the moral law we have particularly in mind, that is, the Ten Commandments. This is not to say that other parts of the law of Moses have no application in preaching the gospel. For example, the death of the animal sacrifices reminds us that death is the penalty for sin. It also foreshadows the substitutionary work of Christ. But the Decalogue has a particular place in evangelism, because it is through these commandments that men are made aware of their sinful state.

That being the case, we have to ask, what is the relationship of man to the moral law? The answer is twofold. Before Adam sinned, he had a wholly positive relationship to the law of God. But after the Fall, that relationship changed dramatically. W. G. T. Shedd, in his *Sermons to the Natural Man*, says, 'The moral law in its own nature, and by the divine ordination, is suited to produce holiness and happiness in the soul of any and every man. It was ordained to life. So far as the purpose of God, and the original nature and character of man, are concerned, the ten commandments are perfectly adapted to fill the soul with peace and purity. In the unfallen creature, they work no wrath, neither are they the strength of sin. If everything in man had remained as it was created, there would have been no need of urging him to "become dead to the law", to be "delivered from the law", and not be "under the law". Had man kept his original righteousness, it could never be said of him that "The strength of sin is the law." On the contrary, there was such a mutual agreement between the unfallen nature of man and the holy law of God, that the latter was the very joy and strength of the former. The commandment was ordained to life, and it was the life and peace of holy Adam.'[2] There is nothing wrong or lacking, therefore, in the law. The fault lies in ourselves, that we are sinners. It is our sinful state that puts us under 'the curse of the law' (Gal. 3:10) and makes us rebel against it. Because we are sinners the law of God is obnoxious to us, and that for two reasons.

The first reason is that the law *is* law, and the sinner does not like being told he is wrong. He does not like absolutes; he prefers standards that are relative, because he can manipulate such standards to serve his own convenience. The absolutes of God's law defy such human ingenuity: they will not appease his conscience and they leave him forever uncomfortable in the presence of God. The second reason is that it is the law *of God*. There is a holiness about the law that will not yield an inch to man's sinfulness. It makes no allowances and accepts no plea in mitigation. It is the unchanging law of an unchanging

God, and is thus as holy and pure as God himself. There are only two ways in which man could come to terms with God's law. The first is if the law could be altered so that it could agree with man's sinful inclination. He would then be happy in his sin because the law would become like his own heart and there would be no conflict between man and law. The second is if man could be changed so that the inclinations and desires of his heart would be in accordance with divine law. Then again there would be no conflict.

The first of these two 'options' is not on. The second is made possible by the gospel of God's grace. But if the gospel is to have this effect, it must be presented in a way that makes clear where man's problem lies. The prime purpose of the gospel is not to make men happy, but to make them righteous in the sight of God. Therefore there is no way the gospel can be preached without the law also being preached. It is only the preaching of the law that shows man what his problem really is, since it is through the law that we become conscious of sin (Rom. 3:20). The law presents us firmly and forcibly with the fact of our own personal sin and guilt (Rom. 3:20; 4:15; 5:13) and having done that, it can lead us in repentance and faith to Christ.

Shedd asks, 'Of what use is the law to a fallen man?' He answers, 'It is preached and forced home in order to detect sin, but not to remove it, to bring men to a consciousness of the evil of their hearts, but not to change their hearts.'[3] In other words, there are limits to what the law can do for us. It forgives none of the sin it reveals; it cannot change the heart it convicts of vileness and depravity;

it saves no lost sinner. Therefore the gospel preacher's responsibility is to use the law *for its prescribed purpose* and then move on quickly to the grace of God in Christ to heal the wound the law has exposed. The purpose of the law is to lead us to Christ.

Misuses of love and law in gospel preaching

There is a preaching of the love of God that can encourage people to continue in their sin. A woman who had been having psychological problems, and was being treated by a psychiatrist, began to attend an evangelical church. She came under conviction of sin as, through the preaching, she saw her sin and guilt. She told her psychiatrist and he was angry and told her to stop attending that church. She did so, and attended another so-called evangelical church. She told them of her experience and of her psychiatrist's anger at her feeling guilty. They said that would not happen in their church because they would surround her with the love of Jesus. To be surrounded with the love of Jesus sounded very spiritual but sadly, in reality, it meant in this case that that church never preached sin or repentance and sinners were never confronted with their real need.

If we are not guilty of this mistake, consider something else that we may well be guilty of. There is a preaching of the law that can discourage sinners from ever seeking Christ. The law is meant to expose the wound so that the balm of the gospel can be applied, but many preachers use the law not so much to expose the wound as to mutilate the body. What I mean is that too often our gospel preaching lacks balance. It is 95% sin, judgement and hell, while the element of good news becomes a two-minute postscript added at the end. You cannot preach the gospel without the law, but the law cannot save. The purpose of preaching the gospel is to save; therefore gospel preaching should be pre-eminently a preaching of Christ and the cross. To reduce that to a postscript is not to preach the gospel at all.

In preparing a gospel sermon we should give a great deal of thought to its balance. It needs both law and grace, and the balance between these is very important. What is the correct balance? It may be that in our days there needs to be a stronger emphasis on God's holiness and law than is common. This aspect has been neglected for so long that men no longer blush at their sin. But having said that, our purpose is not to leave men with a sense of guilt. It is to lead them to the Lord Jesus Christ who in his love and mercy can deal with that guilt.

The correct use of the law in gospel preaching

How, in conclusion then, should we use the law in preaching to the lost? What is the correct use of the law in evangelism? By correct I mean biblical. Romans 3:20 and Galatians 3:21 tell us clearly that the law cannot save, but it is essential in turning a sinner to Christ for salvation. This is because it teaches three things that a man must understand if he is to be truly converted.

1. The law must be used to teach the sinner the holiness of God

One of the basic problems with man is that he does not take sin seriously and this is because he does not take God seriously. There is always the tendency to reduce God to manageable terms. Every system of religion apart from biblical Christianity does this. Tozer wrote, 'Among the sins to which the human heart is prone hardly any other is more hateful to God than idolatry, for idolatry is at bottom a libel on his character. The idolatrous heart assumes that God is other than he is — in itself a monstrous sin — and substitues for the true God one made after his own likeness. Always this god will conform to the image of the one who created it and it will be base or pure, cruel or kind, according to the moral state of the mind from which it emerges.'⁴ It is this thinking that lies behind the saying: 'The God I believe in would never send people to hell.' The only answer to such unbiblical nonsense is to see and appreciate God as the Holy One. As we understand more of God's holiness, we shall inevitably also understand more of man's sinfulness and the necessity of Christ's atoning death. God's holiness is revealed gloriously in the law and the cross.

God is holy and everything he does and instigates is holy. This is seen clearly in the law; its commandments, says Romans 7:12, are 'holy, righteous and good'. The law forbids sin in all its forms, whether it be the vileness of idolatry, murder or adultery, or sin in its more subtle forms of pride and coveteousness. God forbids sin because it is repugnant to his holiness and it pollutes and harms his creation. If the law cannot restrict sin then God will destroy sin. God's wrath and justice are direct consequences of his holiness. God hates sin, as a mother hates a disease that is killing her child.

In preaching the law we must not put before the sinner vague and tentative suggestions as to what God thinks, but clear and precise statements of his attitude to the issues that confront men every day. The law leaves us in no doubt as to the holiness of God, and this confronts the sinner with a huge dilemma. What can he do? His sin condemns him and the holiness of God leaves him with no escape. The law has pushed him into a corner and kicked away the crutches he was depending on. He feels useless and hopeless. But this is the point at which he must arrive if he is to embrace by faith what Christ has done to redeem lost sinners such as he. As Spurgeon said, 'A man is never so near grace as when he begins to feel he can do nothing at all.'

2. *The law must be used to show the sinner the reality of his sin*

Sin was a fact long before the law was given by God and it reaped its grim harvest of death from Adam to Moses. It was while mankind languished in that terrible condition of sin, condemnation and death, that God added the law (Rom. 5:20). 'It was not', says Leon Morris, 'concerned with preventing sin (it was too late for that). Nor was it concerned with salvation from sin (it was too weak for that). The law can only condemn (Rom. 4:15). It was concerned with showing sin for what it is, and it certainly showed magnificently that there was much sin.'[5]

The law shows up sin and prevents man justifying it with pathetic excuses. So when a man excuses his temper as a temperamental weakness, the law of God says, 'No, it is sin.' When a man excuses his sexual lusts as being natural in any red-blooded man, the law says, 'No, it is sin.' Thus the law defines and pin-points sin. The meaning of 'You shall not commit adultery,' cannot be misunderstood. Men can wriggle all they like in discomfort under such a command, but they can never say it was not clear. They can argue all day that such teaching is old-fashioned, and that we must be modern, but they know in their hearts that the commandment is right, especially when it is their own spouse who commits adultery.

The function of the gospel preacher is to use the law to make people see their sin as God sees it. It is to make the sinner think in terms of God's absolute standards, not the ever-changing whims of society. The preacher is always up against fluctuating standards of morality and changing views of what is right and wrong. This fluctuation makes the sinner feel comfortable because what he was doing wrong ten years ago may well now be considered right in the eyes of society. What he is doing wrong now may well be acceptable in five years time. So he thinks, 'What is the problem? I am free to make my own rules.' We must show him that his problem is with the unchanging standards of God; that he will be judged by God, not by trendy TV producers or the editors of tabloid newspapers.

3. The law must be used to point sinners to Christ

We often quote Romans 3:23: 'All have sinned and fall short of the glory of God.' But Paul does not put a full stop after this statement. He continues, 'and are justified freely by his grace through the redemption that came by Christ Jesus' (Rom. 3:24). The whole point of bringing the sinner to a realization of his sin is that he might forsake his works and flee to Christ for deliverance. Thus we should never preach the law without also preaching the redemption that is in Christ. This work of redemption, says the apostle, *justifies* the sinner in the sight of God. Christ has borne the curse of the law, 'becoming a curse for us' (Gal. 3:13), that we might be declared righteous before God.

This imputed righteousness, Paul continues, is free. It cannot be obtained by anything we are or do, for Christ has already paid the whole price. He has 'bought [the church] with his own blood' (Acts 20:28). He has purged our sins 'by himself'; that is, without our aid or co-operation (Heb. 1:3, NKJV). Any attempt to tender our good works or religious offerings to secure our salvation is a negation of the gospel and a rejection of Christ's finished work.

Finally, this redemption is by grace. It is the outcome of God's eternal purpose, motivated by God's eternal love and carried to certain fruition by God's eternal Son. Grace is God's propensity to give eternal riches to those who deserve eternal condemnation, that he might receive eternal glory. The law exposes our devastating poverty so

that we might find unsearchable riches in Christ. Let us be
warned, therefore: if the law of God is on our lips, the love
of God must be in our hearts and the compassion of Christ
in our minds. This is how we should preach the law, for
only thus will God be honoured.

12.
The joy of witness

In the previous three chapters we have been seeing how the preacher should address the unsaved. We come, finally, to a different question: how should the preacher address believers so as to spur them to evangelize? The easy answer is that he should exhort them to this great work, but that is not what I am getting at. No doubt exhortation is both useful and necessary, but it is likely to fall on deaf ears unless something more is done.

The fact is that attitudes to evangelism in the pew will be formed by what is preached from the pulpit. If believers never hear the gospel preached, they will not know how to evangelize themselves. I am suggesting that the greatest stimulus to evangelization that ordinary Christians can receive is to hear the gospel preached regularly and fervently in their own midst. This is not conventional thinking, of course. Many churches make a clear distinction between sermons designed to instruct the saints and those intended to save sinners. The implication is that believers only attend the so-called 'gospel' or 'evangelistic' service to provide a crowd. They do not *need* gospel preaching, they might say, because they are already saved.

They are only there to 'cheer on' the preacher and pray for any unsaved people who may have turned up. They don't really need to listen, because they know it all anyway. They are little more than a 'rent-a-congregation'.

As long as this kind of thinking is prevalent in our churches, evangelism will remain 'dead in the water'. However sternly Christians may be exhorted, they will not evangelize until their hearts are thrilled and enraptured by the gospel. Believers for whom this is true will never willingly miss an opportunity to hear the preaching of God's rich, free grace in Christ. Wild horses will not drag them from a gospel sermon.

A lost enthusiasm

Why is it that we so often lack enthusiasm for the task of evangelism? The fundamental reason has to be that we have lost sight of the glories of the gospel. We have grown cold. This is not difficult to demonstrate. It is usually the newly-converted who are most effective in telling the gospel and bringing newcomers under its sound. The joy of a new discovery is in their hearts and they feel constrained to share it. Theirs is the joy of the woman who has found her lost coin, or the shepherd who has found his lost sheep. Come and 'rejoice with me', they cry to their friends, their neighbours and to all who will listen (Luke 15:6,10).

This freshness and joy do not have to fade with the passing years, but they will certainly do so if we lose sight of the glories of the gospel. How does this happen? It happens when we lose sight of Christ. Paul writes, 'God, who said, "Let light shine out of darkness," made his light shine in our hearts to give us the light of the knowledge of the glory of God in the face of Christ' (2 Cor. 4:6). Paul had been a believer for a long time when he wrote these words, but the reality of which he spoke still thrilled his soul. Do these and similar words of Scripture also fill you with joy and adoration? After all his experiences, rough and smooth, Paul was still gripped by the love of Christ, moved by his compassion, exultant in his riches. He was still a man in love, not with an idea or theory, but with a person.

The cure for a lost enthusiasm

This is where we have to understand the importance of preaching the gospel to believers as well as to the unsaved. Christians have lost the *vision* of Christ because our pulpits have abandoned the *preaching* of Christ. How else will moribund believers recover their desire to make Christ known, except by hearing the preaching of 'Christ and him crucified'? A believer who had just visited Poland said how amazed he was to find congregations 'sitting on the edges of their seats', such was their hunger for the Word of God. 'We never see that here,' he added sadly. Yet only a few miles away from where he lived was a church where the same hunger *was* to be found. What was the secret? Not some charismatic enthusiasm, but a warm, Christ-centred ministry.

We shall not rediscover our enthusiasm for evangelism by setting up training schemes, outreach projects, 'organizing' believers, or by any other human contrivance. The inner fires of love for Christ must be rekindled in our hearts. This will only happen as preachers preach Christ, in all his dying, rising and ascended glory. Whatever may be the subject of a sermon, its object should be Christ. All must be related to him — whether creation, providence, the covenants, the history of the Jews, the psalms, the prophecies, the law, the church, or whatever else provides the topic of the day. Only then can we expect the Holy Spirit to move, for it is his unique work to glorify Christ, taking the things of Christ and revealing them to us (John 16:14). If our preaching lacks Christ, the Spirit of God is left 'waiting in the wings'. Only when Christ is exalted will his church rediscover the great commission to go into all the world and preach the gospel.

The gospel must be preached persistently

It is not easy to preach the gospel when few of our hearers are unsaved. Perhaps the whole congregation is made up of believers. Should we then abandon the gospel and turn to other subjects? Not at all. We must look ahead. The psalmist wrote:

> He who goes out weeping,
>   carrying seed to sow,
> will return with songs of joy,
>   carrying sheaves with him
>
> (Ps. 126:6).

It has been suggested that the tears referred to are not those of sorrow, but rather those caused by the biting winds of seed-time. But unless the sower faces these inclement conditions, the seed will not be sown and the harvest will never come. There is a need for persistence in gospel preaching. If our audience consists of none but Christians, so be it. Let us preach the gospel with such persistence and such fervour that they will begin to think, 'I wish my sister could have heard that sermon'; 'I wish my boss could have been here this morning and hear what we have heard.' Sooner or later, knowing that the gospel will be preached with clarity and power, they will begin to invite their families and their friends.

It is very important that believers know what to expect from the preaching. A university lecturer once invited a visitor from Communist China to attend an evangelical church with him. To his surprise, the visitor agreed to go, since it was Christmastime. Imagine the lecturer's horror when the minister said, 'Since it's Christmas, I decided not to preach a sermon but to have a quiz instead.' This pathetic substitute for preaching left the visitor greatly unimpressed. His one and only experience of a Christian service was nothing short of tragic. This may be an extreme case, but believers sometimes fear to bring their unsaved friends because they cannot be sure what will be preached. The consistent and persistent preaching of Christ will encourage Christians to bring others, and very soon the congregation will no longer be one consisting solely of the saints!

The gospel must be preached fully

We have already seen how Spurgeon and other great preachers held that sinners must be told the 'whole counsel of God', not an edited version of the gospel. If this is true of the unsaved, how much more does it apply to believers! To preach the gospel in terms of God's eternal counsels, his electing love, his sovereign power in salvation and the glory of Christ is to feed God's people as well as to evangelize the lost. Of course, these majestic doctrines must be explained in clear, everyday language, but this is a rich and proper challenge to the preacher.

There is a sense in which every sermon should be a gospel message and an act of instruction also. Any doctrine that does not lead us readily to the person and work of Christ is no doctrine of Scripture. And every doctrine of Scripture will relate in some way to him of whom the Scriptures testify (John 5:39). It is as believers begin to appreciate the profundity of the gospel, as they begin to realize that 'all the treasures of wisdom and knowledge' are hidden in Christ (Col. 2:3), that they will begin to take an interest in the gospel, think about it and share it with their friends. A superficial 'gospel' is not worth passing on.

The gospel must be preached as the privilege that it is

Most Christians today find witness difficult and we are always talking about how hard it is to evangelize. There is no doubt that this is true, but perhaps we ought to talk more of the joy and privilege of the gospel. This privilege is twofold. First of all, we need to understand the unspeakable privilege that has been bestowed upon the believer in Christ. Then, and only then, we shall appreciate the second privilege, that of telling others about the Lord Jesus Christ.

The apostle John exclaims: 'How great is the love the Father has lavished on us, that we should be called children of God! ... Now we are children of God, and what we will be has not yet been made known. But we know that when he appears, we shall be like him, for we shall see him as he is' (1 John 3:1-2). As we read these words, we can almost hear the hushed tones of worship in John's voice. Could any greater privilege even be imagined? No, says Paul, for

> No eye has seen,
>   no ear has heard,
> no mind has conceived
>   what God has prepared for those who love him
>   (1 Cor. 2:9).

The full extent of our privilege in Christ lies beyond our present comprehension. If we understand this, then we shall also understand our second greatest privilege.

Whether preaching from a pulpit, or sharing the gospel in a one-to-one situation, it is an unspeakable privilege to tell men and women, dead in their sins, about God's love in Christ, a mighty Saviour whose name is 'Wonderful,

Counsellor, Mighty God, Everlasting Father, Prince of Peace' (Isa. 9:6). It is our privilege to tell them of the glory of the incarnation, of the beauty of his sinless life, of the death he died to redeem us, of divine justice satisfied, and of the resurrection, ascension and exaltation of Christ; and also to tell them that God demands a response — namely, that we should repent of our sins and come in faith to Christ.

What a joy and privilege to speak of these things! And what joy it is to see the Holy Spirit working in the hearts of sinners — to see indifference and apathy turn to concern, concern to conviction, conviction to salvation. There is nothing like it! To be a soul-winner makes you feel ten feet tall, but at the same time it makes you feel like dust. It is humbling to realize that God condescends to use a sinner like you, with all your faults, to save another soul. Your joy is such that you want to see more souls saved. And there is only one thing that will save sinners — the gospel of Jesus Christ. So you want to tell it with more faithfulness, greater love, greater urgency and greater power. You want success — not just because it makes you feel good, but because God is glorified and sinners are saved from hell.

The soul-winner is a person with a great longing to see God glorified in the salvation of sinners. The difficulties and problems of witness do not put him off; they serve only to enhance his sense of urgency and drive him to the Lord in earnest prayer.

References

Chapter 1 — Go to all nations
1. Sir Leonard Davies, *Welsh Life in the Eighteenth Century,* Country Life, 1939, pp.118-19.
2. A. W. Tozer, *Worship: the Missing Jewel of the Evangelical Church,* Christian Publications, p.14.

Chapter 3 — The hand of the Lord in evangelism
1. William Arnot, *Studies in the Acts,* Kregel, 1978, p.229.
2. A. W. Tozer, *Paths to Power,* Oliphants, 1964, pp.11-15.
3. A. W. Tozer, *The Price of Neglect,* Christian Publications, 1991, p.51.
4. J. Blanchard, *More Gathered Gold,* Evangelical Press, 1988, pp.149-50.
5. J. Blanchard, *Gathered Gold,* Evangelical Press, 1989, p.146.

Chapter 4 — The fruit of evangelism
1. Warren Wiersbe, *On Being a Servant of God,* Word Books, 1993, p.38.

Chapter 5 — Saviour and Lord
1. A. W. Tozer, *I call it Heresy,* Christian Publications, 1974, pp.18-19.
2. D. M. Lloyd-Jones, *Darkness and Light,* Banner of Truth Trust, 1982, p.121.
3. James Montgomery Boice, *Ephesians,* Ministry of Resources Library, 1988, p.147.

Chapter 6 — All things to all men
1. John Stott, *The message of Acts,* IVP, 1990, p.254.

Chapter 7 — Barriers to belief
1. C. H. Spurgeon, *The Soul Winner,* Pilgrim, 1978, p.27.

2. Sinclair Ferguson, *The Sermon on the Mount,* Banner of Truth Trust, 1987, p.155.

Chapter 9 — Gospel preaching
1. Spurgeon, *The Soul Winner,* p.11.
2. C. H. Spurgeon, *Metropolitan Tabernacle Pulpit,* Passmore & Alabaster, 1886, p.346.
3. Spurgeon, *The Soul Winner,* p.17.
4. As above, pp.18-19.
5. Edward Morgan, *John Elias: Life & Letters,* Banner of Truth Trust, 1973, p.354.
6.Spurgeon, *The Soul Winner,* p.20.
7. As above, p.21.
8. As above, p.22.
9. Blanchard, *Gathered Gold,* p.237.
10. D. M. Lloyd-Jones, *Preaching and Preachers,* Hodder & Stoughton, 1971, p.92.
11. As above, p.94.
12. Spurgeon, *The Soul Winner,* p.24.
13. Iain Murray, *Jonathan Edwards,* Banner of Truth Trust, 1987, p.125.
14. As above, p.126.
15. As above, p.128.
16. As above, p.129.
17. As above, p.132.
18. As above, p.133.

Chapter 10 — The gospel preacher
1. Spurgeon, *The Soul Winner,* p.45.
2. Dr & Mrs Howard Taylor, *Biography of Hudson Taylor,* Hodder & Stoughton, 1965, p.79.
3. Andrew Bonar, *Memoir & Remains of Robert Murray M'Cheyne,* Wm Middleton, 1844, p.149.
4. As above, p.150.
5. As above, p.250.
6. As above.
7. Spurgeon, *The Soul Winner,* p.76.
8. Lloyd-Jones, *Preaching and Preachers,* p.9.
9. C. H. Spurgeon, quoted in *The Banner of Truth* magazine, April 1960.
10. Spurgeon, *The Soul Winner,* p.57.
11. John Calvin, *Commentary on John,* Baker Book House, 1979, p.125.
12. As above.
13. John Brown, *Discourses and Sayings of our Lord,* Banner of Truth Trust, 1967, vol. 1, p.35.

Chapter 11 — Evangelism and the law of God
1. J. I. Packer, *Evangelism and the Sovereighty of God,* IVP, 1961, p.61.
2. W. G. T. Shedd, *Sermons to the Natural Man,* Banner of Truth Trust, 1977, pp.232-3.
3. As above, p.175.
4. A. W. Tozer, *The Knowledge Of the Holy,* James Clarke, 1965, p.11.
5. Leon Morris, *Romans,* Eerdmans, 1988, p.240.